AF594360

Praise for *Glorious Encounters with Mary*

In *Glorious Encounters with Mary*, praying the Glorious Mysteries takes on a renewed brilliance. Maria Gallagher combines Sacred Scripture, magisterial documents, the lives of the saints, and her own life to form a dazzling mosaic of faith, hope, and love. Reading about relationships in Maria's life set against the background of her deep faith, one cannot help but consider one's own experiences that have brought sorrow, joy, and, ultimately, glorious victory. Her resilient love for God, His Church, and her family shines through on every page. Her willingness to share from the heart and her own consecration to Our Lady sing a hymn of love for all to hear. This is a must-read for all who seek a relationship with the heavenly Mother God has given us.

— **Most Reverend William J. Waltersheid,**
Auxiliary Bishop of Pittsburgh.

In her follow-up to *Joyful Encounters with Mary: A Woman's Guide to Living the Mysteries of the Rosary.* Maria Gallagher shares a personal story of how each Glorious Mystery has been relevant in her life, offers ways for readers to grow in the virtue associated with that mystery, and profiles a saint who exemplifies that virtue. Readers will learn more about faith, hope, love of God, devotion to Mary, and the desire for eternal happiness, and be introduced to saintly role models. Maria writes to encourage those who are new to devotion to the Blessed Mother and praying the Rosary, those who pray the Rosary daily, and everyone in between. Her personal testimony of prayers answered and graces received is powerful. Her willingness to share the painful chapters of her own life and how God brought good out of them is inspiring. *Glorious Encounters with Mary* is recommended for anyone who wishes to learn more about the Glorious Mysteries of the Rosary or to deepen their relationship with Jesus and Mary.

— **Patrice Fagnant-MacArthur,** author of *The Fruits of the Mysteries of the Rosary.*

Glorious Encounters With Mary is another beautiful Marian account created by author Maria Gallagher and her continued contemplation of the Blessed Mother. By incorporating her personal experiences, stories from the saints, and a walk through each of the Glorious Mysteries, Maria encourages the reader to have a personal relationship with Our Lady while falling in love with the Rosary if they haven't already.

— **Andrea Bear**, author of *Grieving Daughters' Club* and co-host of the "Mourning Glory" podcast.

Maria Gallagher has an engaging writing style, particularly when she incorporates stories from her own life and the lives of saints to bring the mysteries of the Rosary to life. *Glorious Encounters with Mary* details the Glorious Mysteries of the Rosary, and allows readers to grow in virtue themselves, particularly with the "Personal Reflection" questions at the end of each chapter. This would be the ideal book to bring to church on a First Saturday, when the faithful are instructed to go to Confession, receive Holy Communion, say five decades of the Rosary, and spend 15 minutes with Our Lady meditating on the mysteries of the Rosary.

— **Amanda Lauer**, award-winning author of the *Heaven Intended* Civil War series.

Glorious Encounters with Mary teaches us that praying with Mary leads us into a deeper trust in God. Maria Gallagher shares how the personal intimate moments of her own life drew her closer to Mary in the Glorious Mysteries of the Rosary. Her testimony inspires and challenges us to reflect on our own moments encountering the Glory and Power of God.

— **Shelly Henley Kelly**, "Of Sound Mind and Spirit" writer and podcaster.

In *Glorious Encounters with Mary*, Maria Gallagher seamlessly weaves together the significance of each of the Glorious Mysteries of the Rosary with stories from her own life, stories of the saints, and practical tips and resources to grow in virtue and faith. The result is a beautiful tapestry of grace and inspiration, leading us to the heart of the Blessed Mother and her Son. Maria's writing style is incredibly poignant and relatable. Even if we don't share her same experiences, she's so open and honest, we can't help but feel a connection that draws us even deeper into this powerful read!

— **Claire McGarry,** author of *Grace in Tension: Discover Peace with Martha and Mary.*

Maria Gallagher has beautifully woven elements of her own story and relationship with Mary into *Glorious Encounters with Mary.* Thought-provoking personal reflections are included at the end of each chapter, allowing readers the opportunity to grow deeper in relationship with not only Mary, but also Jesus. The rich history included throughout the book also provides readers with additional insight into the life of Mary from various perspectives, all while making the connection to each of the virtues and mysteries of the Rosary.

— **Jennifer Thomas,** co-host of the "Mourning Glory" podcast.

In *Glorious Encounters with Mary,* Maria Gallagher once again creates a spiritual retreat that moves, inspires, and uplifts the reader. While revealing some of the most difficult moments of her life, she recounts how Our Blessed Mother and several other Saints have led her ever closer to our Lord, helping her to grow in virtue, trust, and holiness, even along a rocky path. Maria has an incredible gift of finding that just right word or phrase that resonates, perfectly capturing what can be difficult to articulate. This book not only delights — it fortifies us for our own challenges on the journey.

— **Bonnie Finnerty,** pro-life speaker, writer, and advocate.

Enter into the Glorious Mysteries of the Rosary with Maria Gallagher as your guide. You'll contemplate the significance of these mysteries in your own life, along with the lives of familiar saints and Maria's own reflections. This book opens the door to a deeper devotion to the Rosary.

— **Barb Szyszkiewicz,** editor at CatholicMom.com and author of *The Handy Little Guide to Prayer.*

Glorious Encounters with Mary

A Guide to Living the Mysteries of the Rosary

Maria V. Gallagher

author of

Joyful Encounters with Mary: A Woman's Guide to Living the Mysteries of the Rosary

© 2024 Maria V. Gallagher. All rights reserved.

Available from:
Marian Helpers Center
Stockbridge, MA 01263
Prayerline: 1-800-804-3823
Orderline: 1-800-462-7426
ShopMercy.org

Websites:
Marian.org
TheDivineMercy.org
DivineMercyPlus.org

Library of Congress Control Number: 2024937034

ISBN: 978-1-59614-623-5

Imprimi Potest:
Very Rev. Chris Alar, MIC, Provincial Superior
The Blessed Virgin Mary, Mother of Mercy Province
May 9, 2024
Solemnity of the Ascension of the Lord

Nihil Obstat:
Robert A. Stackpole, STD, Censor Deputatus
May 9, 2024

Note: The *Nihil Obstat* and corresponding *Imprimi Potest* are not a certification that those granting it agree with the contents, opinions, or statements expressed in the work. Instead, they merely confirm that the work contains nothing contrary to faith and morals.

Scripture texts in this work are taken from the *New American Bible, revised edition* © 2010, 1991, 1986, 1970 Confraternity of Christian Doctrine, Washington, D.C. and are used by permission of the copyright owner. All Rights Reserved. No part of the New American Bible may be reproduced in any form without permission in writing from the copyright owner.

Excerpts from the English translation of the *Catechism* of the Catholic Church for use in the United States of America Copyright © 1994, United States Catholic Conference, Inc. — Libreria Editrice Vaticana. Used with Permission. English translation of the *Catechism* of the Catholic Church: Modifications from the Editio Typica copyright © 1997, United States Conference of Catholic Bishops — Libreria Editrice Vaticana.

This book is dedicated to my brilliant
and beautiful daughter,
Gabriella,
who lights up the world
with her very presence.

You have taught me more
than I could have ever taught you,
and my love for you is boundless.

TABLE OF CONTENTS

A great sign appeared in the sky,
a woman clothed with the sun,
with the moon under her feet,
and on her head a crown of twelve stars.

— Revelation 12:1

INTRODUCTION
Glorious Encounters with Mary

Sixteen years.

When I type that line, I am in awe of the God Whom I serve and the Almighty Father Who has been ever faithful to me. For, after 16 years of waiting and wondering, contemplating and commiserating, I discovered that God had answered the most precious prayer I had held for so long within my heart.

It was a glorious moment — an experience I shared with the Blessed Mother. For a long time ago, I consecrated myself to the Immaculate Heart of Mary, and, ever since, my life has been intertwined with that of the mother of Jesus. It has been quite an adventure, and I recommend consecration to everyone who wants to develop a deeper relationship with both Mary and Jesus. Through this consecration, I was able to give myself entirely to Jesus through Mary's Immaculate Heart. This meant relinquishing all my goods — both temporal and spiritual — to Mary to use as she sees fit. It was a critical moment in my life, and I credit it with transforming my soul in a most powerful and beautiful way.

In the wake of my consecration, I now offer my prayers, good works, and sacrifices each day to the

Blessed Mother, to do with as she wishes. God pours His grace into Mary's hands, and she, in turn, applies that grace wherever she chooses. In effect, I abandon myself to Mary — and land safely and snugly in Jesus' arms.[1]

In my first book, *Joyful Encounters with Mary: A Woman's Guide to Living the Mysteries of the Rosary* (Marian Press, 2022), I examined how the Joyful Mysteries of the Rosary can be lived out in an individual woman's life. In discovering those connections, a woman can draw closer to Mary and, in turn, draw closer to Jesus, since Mary always leads us to her beloved Son.

After the book was published, I heard from readers who longed for more — a deeper relationship with the Blessed Mother. These dedicated readers also encouraged me to explore additional mysteries of the Rosary — to find more meeting places where we could all experience Mary's profound love. With loving persistence, they urged me to write a follow-up book to continue the Marian adventure.

In light of the 16-year-old prayer that recently had been answered in my life, I felt drawn to the Glorious Mysteries and the promise and the possibility they held. I knew my experience with God and the Blessed Mother had indeed been glorious, and I wanted to share that incredible happiness with the world.

While I cannot guarantee that your long-standing prayer will be answered in the manner in which you wish, I can say that Mary and her Son will never abandon you. You can have peace, resting safely and sweetly in their all-encompassing embrace. With Mary and Jesus by your side, you can discover glories that you may not have noticed in the past.

I designed this book for a variety of individuals:

- People who are curious about the Blessed Mother, but do not know much about her.
- People who already have a strong devotion to Mary, but want to strengthen their relationship with her.
- People who have never prayed the Glorious Mysteries of the Rosary.
- People who have been taught the Rosary, but pray it infrequently.
- People who have a daily devotion to the Rosary, including the Glorious Mysteries.

Glorious Encounters with Mary: A Guide to Living the Mysteries of the Rosary offers personal reflections and scriptural meditations to enhance your appreciation of the Glorious Mysteries. It also provides some strategies for growing in the various virtues associated with each mystery. You will also learn about various saints who experienced a special connection with the Blessed Mother.

My hope and prayer are that, in reading *Glorious Encounters with Mary*, you will come to see the ribbon that runs through your life and connects you with the Blessed Virgin Mary. May that connection be a source of strength and encouragement to you as you journey through life.

Personal Reflections

1. What comes to mind when you think about the Glorious Mysteries of the Rosary?
2. Which is your favorite Glorious Mystery, and why do you think that is the case?
3. What do you share in common with the Blessed Mother?
4. Think back to a time in your life that you would describe as "glorious." What specifically made it so?

CHAPTER 1
Rising from the Ashes

It seemed to come about all of a sudden — but, in truth, my passage from a rather carefree young woman to a victim of violence was, in fact, a gradual process. I fell hard for a handsome stranger and assumed that, because he showed an interest in me, he was the man God had chosen to accompany me through life. I dated him for nearly two years, thinking that the only logical next step was marriage.

I believed with all my heart that I was living out my life's vocation when I said "I do."

Looking back, there were warning signs — a disrespectful comment here, a disregard for my feelings there. Slowly, seemingly imperceptibly, my confidence eroded and my self-image shattered. I lost my identity and, at times, I also lost my connection with Christ. I was adrift in a sea of misery, unable to see that Jesus and His mother Mary wanted to extend a life preserver to me. Isolated and confused, I was alone in my sorrow.

At that time, I felt that being an abuse victim was my lot in life. I believed that I had made a series of poor decisions, sending my life off-course.

I perceived, wrongly, that I deserved my fate and that I was doomed to live with the constant threat of violence. While the physical abuse was painful, it was the emotional abuse that took the greatest toll on my psyche.

I had forgotten that I was an adopted daughter of a King — made so through my Baptism when I was a baby. I had lost the sense of my inherent dignity and worth. I believed the lie that I was worthless, and I even believed, quite wrongly, that I was undeserving of life.

Each day was a monumental struggle against fear, desperation, and pessimism. I could no longer feel God's presence with me — it was as if He had left the building and I was fending for myself. I abandoned prayer, thinking that God did not want to hear from me. Previously, I had prayed to be delivered from abuse — failing to recognize the fact that the only way to guarantee my safety was to leave my current living arrangement.

My breaking point came on an autumn evening when I ran out of my apartment with my baby in my arms and sought safe shelter with an acquaintance nearby. It would take a long time for me to permanently escape the abuse, but that night was definitely a turning point. I finally felt as if I had wrestled back control of my life and I discovered a power that I did not know I had.

As a result of the abuse, I harbored a feeling of being dead inside. I also thought that my soul was headed to Hell with no possibility of redemption. I felt immersed in a psycho-drama that was destined for an unhappy ending.

But, ultimately, I found new life in Christ. It was like a personal resurrection, as I rediscovered the endless love God held for me. I arose from the ashes of abuse as a new person — wiser, more focused, and more understanding of God's will for my life.

I believe the Blessed Mother was a witness to my transformation, as well as a catalyst for it. She illuminated for me a path to restoration and wholeness, a place of grace and empowerment. In deciding that I would devote myself to her, I found a forever friend who would lead me to an avenue of healing.

My resurrection took a lot longer than three days. I believe my own stubbornness caused me to put up obstacles which hindered my healing. Once I decided to let go and let God, my life began to turn around.

It was not an easy transition — the wounds of abuse were deep. But I discovered a wellspring of hope in Mary and Jesus and that helped to set my life aright. My friends marveled at the positive, life-affirming changes they saw in me. I regained my sense of self and rediscovered the hope of my youth.

With God's grace, I grew spiritually to the point where I could again see the hand of God in my life.

I availed myself of a retreat where I found profound joy and affirmation of my identity as an adopted child of God. I began to attend Mass — either in person or virtually — each day, and discovered much solace there.

I came to realize the fundamental truth that Jesus wanted me to love myself and, once I had accomplished that challenging feat, I could love my neighbor. I also accepted the fact that God had never wanted me to undergo abuse, and that such violence and mistreatment go against everything that He stands for.

My new life included a network of supportive friends … unbelievably encouraging co-workers … and a church family that has prayed me through difficulties time and time again. I have to say that, at times, I feel as if I am experiencing a slice of Heaven on earth — a long way from the days when I thought my soul would be trapped in Hell for all eternity. While I work against the presumption that I am destined for Heaven, I also recognize that, with God's grace, I have a fighting chance of living with Him forever in paradise.

If you have suffered abuse of any kind, know that Jesus and His mother Mary stand ready to assist you to recover from your pain. You might consider reaching out to organizations such as Catholic Charities for emotional and psychological support. You, too, can experience a kind of personal resurrection where your faith in yourself, your neighbor, and God are restored.

Please rest assured of my prayers as you begin, or continue, your healing journey.

Personal Reflections

1. What has been a "resurrection experience" in your life?
2. If you have not had such an experience, what do you think is blocking your path?
3. Reflect on your life and name the occasions when you have had a heavenly experience.
4. What one thing can you do this week to draw closer to Mary and Jesus?

CHAPTER 2
The Resurrection of Jesus

Each year I am filled with profound elation at the thought of the Resurrection of Jesus. It fills my heart with happiness to know that Jesus has conquered death and has brought the promise of new life to His followers.

The basis of my belief can be found in scripture. In reading the account from Matthew's gospel, I can experience the Resurrection through the eyes of the women who came to Jesus' tomb. We read:

> Then the angel said to the women in reply, "Do not be afraid! I know that you are seeking Jesus the Crucified. He is not here, for he has been raised just as he said. Come and see the place where he lay" (Mt 28:5-6).

It is altogether fitting that the angel instructs the women not to be afraid. So often in life, when Jesus does the unexpected, I find myself fearful. What I need to realize is that Jesus acts from a place of love and that His actions — even the unexpected ones — are based on what is best for us.

The angel also informs the women that they cannot keep the news of Christ's Resurrection to themselves — they must immediately share it with others:

> "Then go quickly and tell His disciples, 'He has been raised from the dead, and He is going before you to Galilee; there you will see him.' Behold, I have told you." Then they went away quickly from the tomb, fearful yet overjoyed, and ran to announce this to his disciples (Mt 28:7-8).

In this way, the women are called upon to evangelize, to spread the Good News of Jesus' new life after death. We, too, are commissioned to evangelize, to share the message of hope and transformation which are found in Christ's Resurrection. It is part of our baptismal calling to spread the good news that Jesus entrusted to us.

The Resurrection is an event that we share with the Blessed Mother. Saints throughout the centuries have commented on the glorious occasion of Jesus' appearance to His Mother after His Resurrection.

For instance, Pope St. John Paul II stated:

> The Gospels mention various appearances of the risen Christ, but not a meeting between Jesus and His Mother. This silence must not lead to the conclusion that after the Resurrection Christ did not appear to

> Mary; rather it invites us to seek the reasons why the Evangelists made such a choice.[2]

The pontiff offered his own reason why the Gospel writers chose not to chronicle Jesus' appearance to His mother after the Resurrection:

> [T]his can perhaps be attributed to the fact that such a witness would have been considered too biased by those who denied the Lord's Resurrection, and therefore not worthy of belief.[3]

It is also reasonable to believe that the Evangelists simply did not mention all of Jesus' many post-Resurrection appearances. Saint John Paul II makes the case that not everything that occurred in the lives of Jesus and Mary is recorded in the Gospels. But it makes sense that Jesus, given His profound love for His mother and His close relationship with her, would have met with her immediately after His Resurrection.

And what a glorious encounter that must have been! Imagine the incomparable joy of the reunion between mother and Son — especially in light of His excruciatingly painful death. Indeed, we can surmise that Mary experienced a glimpse of Heaven when she saw Jesus in His resurrected state. After her intense suffering during the Crucifixion, the Blessed Mother could once again gaze upon Jesus, knowing that He had triumphed over tragedy.

Saint Ignatius of Loyola also believed that Mary was foremost among the people Jesus visited after His Resurrection:

> First, He appeared to the Virgin Mary. This, although it is not said in Scripture, is included in saying that He appeared to so many others, because Scripture supposes that we have understanding, as it is written: "Are you also without understanding?"[4]

Meanwhile, St. Bridget of Sweden, who achieved acclaim for her visions, offered this assessment of the Resurrection:

> When the third day came, it brought bewilderment and anxiety to the disciples. The women going to the tomb to anoint the body of Jesus sought Him and could not find Him. The Apostles were gathered together in their fear, guarding the doors. Then, surely, though we are not told of this in the Gospels, Mary spoke of the Resurrection of her son, that he had truly risen from death, that He was alive again in all His humanity, no more subject to death, risen to an eternal glory.
>
> We read that Mary Magdalene and the apostles were first to see the risen Christ. But we may believe that Mary His mother knew of His rising before all others, and

> that she was the first to see Him. It was Mary in her lowliness who first gave praise and adoration to the risen Christ.[5]

Twentieth-century priest Fr. John Hardon, S.J., considered by the Church for sainthood, also made a strong case for the contention that the Blessed Mother saw Jesus in all His glory shortly after the Resurrection:

> It is not only a pious opinion that the Risen Savior first appeared to His Mother on Easter Sunday. No less than six Doctors of the Church, including Sts. Ambrose, Anselm, and Albert the Great held that Our Lady was the first witness of the Resurrection.[6]

Father Hardon further argued that a strong connection exists between the Annunciation, when the Archangel Gabriel announced that Mary would conceive and bear a Son through the power of the Holy Spirit, and the Resurrection, when that very Son rose from the dead.[7]

Mary represents the human race. At the point of the Annunciation, the human race needed a Savior. At the moment of the Resurrection, Jesus proved He was the Messiah for whom humanity had been longing.

Furthermore, Fr. Hardon contended that Mary received her vocation as mother of God at the

Annunciation, whereas at the Resurrection she saw the Gospel fulfilled in her Son conquering death and opening the gates of Heaven to those who believe in Him and follow His Word.

The Resurrection represents a triumph of Christ over sin and division. It only makes sense that the Blessed Mother shares in the glory of that Resurrection, which ushered in a new era for humanity.

We should never become so despondent that we forget the joy of the Resurrection, the most glorious event in the history of the Church. In times of difficulty, when we may even be in danger of despair, let us ponder the Resurrection and the great hope it carries with it for our salvation and for the salvation of the world.

Personal Reflections

1. In what ways have you found it challenging to believe in Christ's Resurrection?
2. How does the Resurrection give you hope?
3. What connections do you draw between the Annunciation and the Resurrection?
4. What would you like to ask Jesus for today?

CHAPTER 3
Growing in Virtue: Faith

It was a phone call which took me completely off-guard and which ushered in a new phase of life for my family.

A police officer from a suburb of my hometown was calling my office to inform me that my 79-year-old mother had been taken to the hospital. She had driven to the suburb and had run out of gas in the middle of busy daytime traffic. When the police discovered her, she seemed dehydrated and confused and they had summoned an ambulance.

I knew in that moment that God had been watching over my mother, working through others to get her the medical attention she needed. While I was obviously concerned about my mother's health, I was also grateful to the Lord for His kindness and mercy toward her. An empty gas tank is not normally a cause for celebration, but in this case it had been the catalyst for care for my mother. And for that I was exceedingly thankful.

The incident reminded me of something that had happened years before, on the eve of the Fourth of July. My parents, who had been out on an errand, were driving home when, within a block of our house, their sedan was struck by a driver under the influence of alcohol. Miraculously, my mother and father survived the crash, but my Mom had suffered a broken pelvis, leaving her unable to walk. An emergency squad had transported her to a nearby hospital, where she was spending the night. My father did not suffer physical injuries, but he was shaken up — so emotionally distraught that he barely spoke.

I remember sitting in the basement of our rented house, wondering how our family would manage this crisis. My mother was our rock, and even though I was in college, I was so incredibly dependent on her. She was the one who made sure supper was on the table. She chauffeured us to our appointments, and made sure we had clean clothes to wear to them. With Mom now in the hospital, I seriously did not know how we would survive.

When my mother returned home, she did so in a wheelchair. We converted the downstairs den into a makeshift bedroom. My father, sister, and I were now the caregivers, with my mother the reluctant patient.

Gradually, through what I saw as the miracle of physical therapy, my mother graduated from the wheelchair to a walker. While she was in the hospital, a priest had paid her a visit and given her Holy Communion — the first time she had received the Blessed Sacrament in years. It was amazing in the months afterward to see her put forth such effort to approach the altar on Sundays to receive Jesus into her body and soul. Seeing her hobbling along with her walker brought me to tears.

In my mother, I saw not only a fighter, but a mirror image of Jesus. In overcoming the disability caused by the car crash, my mother had experienced her own type of resurrection. It was as if, during that challenging time, God had planted a seed which caused my mother to blossom. She returned to the sacrament of her youth, grateful to be united with Jesus once again.

Now I was faced with a new crisis involving my mother. I knew that I needed to be by my mother's bedside, so I set out on a journey back to my hometown. When I arrived at the hospital, a nurse suggested that I apply for family leave from my job, knowing that it would take some time for me to deal with my mother's medical crisis.

She originally had been diagnosed with an infection, but the medical staff suspected that she was afflicted with bladder cancer. She was too frail for a biopsy — over the course of a year, her weight had plummeted and she was a shadow of her former self. However, it should be duly noted that she was as feisty as ever and not ready to surrender her fight for life.

The medical team determined that she needed to be transferred to a skilled nursing facility for follow-up care. But my mother wanted to return to her rented home, and initially resisted any notion of living anywhere else.

I besieged Heaven with prayers that my mother would accept the hospital's recommendation. Each day when I visited her, she seemed immovable on the issue of her living arrangements.

But I knew in my heart that God was in control — and I had faith that He would come through for us. The nurses noted that my mother was keenly interested in everything her doctor had to say. They thought that, if the doctor spoke to her, she might be willing to follow his instructions.

After several days, my mother finally acceded to her doctor's directive. She did an about-face and reluctantly agreed to move into the rehabilitation center. Her assent was an answer to my most urgent prayer.

Since I had to return to my job in another state, I had to have faith that God would take care of my mother in the skilled nursing facility. Moving her in was a leap into the great unknown — but I distinctly felt that that was God's call for both of us at that time.

After she took a brief trip back to the hospital, a caring nurse contacted me, encouraging me to try to persuade my mother to submit to hospice care. The nurse told me my mother was not going to get any better, and that it was likely that she would only live another six months.

The news was distressing and yet, here again, I felt that Christ was with us. I believed that the hospice care was part of God's plan for my mother and that, through it, she would receive the comfort and solace she so desperately needed.

Just a few weeks later, I received the call I had been dreading. The hospice nurse informed me that my mother was near death. Yet again, God showed His power, bringing a chaplain who sat with my mother during her final hours, reciting Marian prayers which gave her peace. I was too far away to arrive at my mother's bedside before she died, but God made sure that she was not alone.

During my mother's sickness and subsequent death, I discovered a faith that I did not realize I had — one that trusted the good Lord to take care of both of us, even in the most trying of times. When my mother died, I lost the person who loved me most. Even though it has been more than a decade since she left this earth, I still long to call her on my cellphone and discuss the latest happenings in my life.

I have come to realize that that longing is actually a longing for God. I can call upon Him any time of the day or night, and He will listen to me. While I will always miss my mother, in her absence I have a greater appreciation for the protection God provides to me.

Tragedy can compel us to grow in faith. But it is not the only means by which we can enhance this virtue. Here are a few ways to increase our faith in the Almighty:

- Pray for the gift of greater faith. Sometimes to receive, we need to ask. If we humbly beseech the Lord for the goodness of faith, we might be surprised by the ways that He answers our heartfelt prayer.

- Write down a list of prayer requests. Three months later, review your list. How has God responded to your pleas?

- Take time each morning to make a Spiritual Communion, asking Jesus to come into your heart. The more you unite your soul to Him, the more likely you are to discover daily miracles in your life.

- Find a spiritual director. This is a priest, sister, or trained layperson who can help to guide you in your spiritual life. If a spiritual director is not available at your parish, you may be able to find one by contacting your local diocesan office for a list of recommendations.

Growth in the virtue of faith can be quite the challenging adventure. In order to experience genuine growth, our faith must be tested. But Mary and Jesus stand ever ready to assist us in times of doubt and darkness. Rely on them to shine a light which you can follow in the darkest of spaces.

Personal Reflections

1. Think back to a time when you experienced a death in your family or among your friend group. How did that loss affect your faith in God?
2. What obstacles to faith do you currently face?
3. Would your current faith move mountains? If not, what can you do to change that?
4. Who do you know who has exhibited a strong faith, and how has that example affected you?

CHAPTER 4
Saintly Encounter: St. Rita of Cascia

When my daughter was little, whenever I would take her to her ballet lesson in Philadelphia, I would pass by the National Shrine of St. Rita of Cascia. It is a beloved spot in southeastern Pennsylvania, a sacred haven for pilgrims who travel from throughout the world to learn more about this patron of impossible cases.

As Pope St. John Paul II stated:

> Rita offers her rose to each of you: in receiving it spiritually, strive to live as witnesses to a hope that never disappoints and as missionaries of a life that conquers death. Let it symbolize a life sustained by passionate love for the Lord Jesus, a life capable of responding to suffering and to thorns with forgiveness and the total gift of self, in order to spread everywhere the good odor of Christ through a consistently lived proclamation of the Gospel.[8]

Margherita Lotti was born in a small village in the republic of Cascia (present-day Italy) in 1381.[9] Her name can be translated as "pearl," but she was referred to by the nickname Rita. She formed a bond with the Augustinian nuns who resided at St. Mary Magdalene Monastery, and she felt she had a calling for the religious life. However, her parents intervened and arranged for her to marry a man named Paolo Mancini. Rita and Paolo formed a family, welcoming two sons.

Not long after, tragedy struck, as Paolo became a victim of murder. Rather than hold hatred in her heart, however, Rita forgave her husband's killers and urged her sons to follow suit. Tragedy arrived at Rita's doorstep yet again when both sons died of illness.

At this point, Rita turned to God with renewed fervor, seeking a vocation as a nun in the Augustinian convent. But she faced sizeable obstacles. The community turned down her request for entrance, noting that the rest of her family had not forgiven her husband's murderers. Complicating matters was the fact that members of a family who served as a rival to the Mancinis lived in the convent. As a result, the nuns surmised that Rita's very presence would sow the seeds of discord within the monastery.

But Rita was, by nature, a peacemaker. She proved it by convincing both her husband's family and the rival family to sign a peace accord which put the hostilities to rest once and for all. The scene of the two families embracing can be seen in a fresco in the Church of St. Francis in Cascia.

As a result of her successful peacemaking mission, Rita won acceptance into the Augustinian convent at age 36. She lived a life of peaceful obedience, prayer, and contemplation until 1442. On Good Friday of that year, she offered to share in the pain of Christ's suffering and consequently received a thorn from the crown which had pierced His forehead. The thorn resulted in an open wound on her own forehead which she bore until the day of her death in 1457.

A few months prior to her departure from this earth, a relative visited her, asking her if, during her sickness, there was anything she wanted. Rita ended up requesting a rose from her family garden — a curious request, given the fact that she made the request in January, during the dark days of winter. The relative discovered a rose miraculously peeking out from beneath the snow and presented it to Rita, who took it as a sign of salvation for her deceased husband and sons. With the arrival of this precious floral gift, Rita had confidence that she would be reunited with her family in Heaven.

Rita's first miracle occurred not long after her death. Her body had been placed in a simple coffin made of wood, and a carpenter who had been partially paralyzed stated, "If only I were well, I would have prepared a place more worthy of you." In short order, his paralysis lifted, and he prepared an elaborate casket for Rita.[10] Interestingly enough, she was never buried because so many people wanted to view the body of the "Peacemaker of Cascia." Her body, still incorrupt, can be viewed in Cascia's Basilica of St. Rita.

This beloved saint and miracle worker shares much in common with the Blessed Mother. She was humble, accepting that she was but a tool in God's almighty hand. She was courageous, persevering through tremendous trials. She was also a woman of great hope, seeing the possibility of peace where others saw only discord and strife.

Saint Rita has come to be known as a patroness of victims of abuse, widows, parents, and those experiencing marital difficulties. Many times I have turned to this legendary saint in times of trouble, and I have always found in her a listening ear. I am sure that, over the years, she has enabled me to experience a resurrection of sorts amid darkness and even despair. And for that she has earned a special place among my "Saint friends."

Personal Reflections

1. What, if anything, did you know about St. Rita of Cascia prior to reading this chapter?
2. Which "impossible cause" could you give over to St. Rita at this time in your life?
3. Is there someone you need to forgive from the depths of your heart? What is stopping you?
4. Are there friends or relatives that you believe could use St. Rita's intercession today?

CHAPTER 5
Hope After Death

I remember the last phone conversation I had with my father. This was five years before my mother's death. It was a glorious day — a goal I had been working toward for quite some time finally had materialized. I wanted to share my elation immediately with my parents. But they were hundreds of miles away, back in my hometown. I could not just pop over and uncork a bottle of sparkling cider to share with them. So I turned to my cellphone and hoped that we could bridge the miles for a jubilant cellular celebration.

I noticed that my father was unusually quick to hand off the phone to my Mom. I barely had gotten my words out when he said, "Let me get your mother." It seemed a little odd, but I was so eager to share my news that I shrugged off my father's reticence. I just figured we could have an in-depth conversation later.

The very next day I received a panicked call from my mother. My father had collapsed during the night and had been transported by ambulance to the hospital. The whole time I had known my father, he had never been hospitalized, so this was jarring news. Given the gravity of the situation, I told my mother it would be good to contact a priest to administer to my father the Sacrament of Anointing of the Sick.

"Can you do that?" she asked.

I had not lived in my hometown for several years, and I was not exactly up-to-date on priest assignments. But, with a quick prayer for help from the Almighty and a few phone calls, I was able to arrange for a priestly visit for my father.

Despite the comfort which the Sacrament brought, I was still nervous. My protector, my champion, my cheerleader was incapacitated, and it frightened me. I knew I would need to journey back to my hometown to see him so I could make my own assessment of the state of his health.

It was quite the lonely drive as I made my way to the hospital. When I finally arrived, I was puzzled by the way that his head now wobbled when he tried to talk. My father did not drink alcohol, but he appeared as if he were intoxicated. He no longer had the steadiness and surety that he had been known for.

The man who had been so gifted at coming up with clever sayings and amateur song lyrics was now struggling mightily for words. At one point, he kept saying, "I want to … I want to … I want to …"

Trying to be helpful, I interjected, "Go to the bathroom?" And he laughed. It was a rare moment of levity in an otherwise somber situation.

The doctors were perplexed — they really did not know what was going on with him, medically speaking. I struggled to make sense of the entire situation. Why had God allowed this to happen? How were my mother, sister, and I expected to cope?

At one point, a doctor suggested that my father might have suffered a diabetic stroke. While the diagnosis made sense, it still came as a surprise since, prior to that point, my father's diabetes had been undiagnosed. He had not been to the doctor for a while, so his medical problems had gone undetected.

Still, I felt confident that my father could recover. He was transferred to a rehabilitation center, where he began receiving Holy Communion on a regular basis. This was a pleasant surprise since, prior to his receiving the Anointing of the Sick, my father had not received Communion for 42 years, since his wedding day. He was a faithful Sunday Mass-goer — he just did not ever join the Communion line. I considered his resumption of the practice of receiving Holy Communion to be nothing short of miraculous.

I had to return to my job, so I was forced to leave my hometown once again. My mother would provide me with daily updates on my father's health.

In addition to the verbal and cognitive challenges caused by the stroke, my father was also battling prostate cancer. He carried his cross with courage and incredible emotional strength.

Less than two months later, I received a call from the intensive care unit of a hospital in my hometown. It just so happened that I was in my local Eucharistic Adoration chapel, praying for my father, when the nurse called. The call had gone to my voicemail as I completed my adoration hour. I will never forget exiting the chapel, cellphone to my ear, listening to the message. I called the hospital back and learned that my father's heart had stopped, but that he had been revived.

I returned to my home and began to cry in anguish. I knew this was a moment when my family desperately needed prayer support, so I emailed an urgent prayer request to a prayer chain to which I belonged. With prayers ascending, I planned my trip back to my hometown to see my father.

Again, I was quite nervous as I drove the seven-and-a-half hours to my parents' home. When I arrived, I discovered a note from my mother, saying that she was at the hospital. At that moment, a feeling of terror flowed through me. I realized that I would probably be visiting my father for the last time.

When I arrived at the ICU and approached his bedside, I began talking to him but immediately sensed he was not cognizant of my presence. A nurse had told me my father was the sickest patient in the unit and I felt a pang of sorrow as my mother stroked his hand. My sister was also there, and I asked her to pray a Rosary aloud for him.

Once we finished the Rosary, I could see that my mother was exhausted. She had not had dinner yet, and I was concerned about her stamina. I persuaded her to pick up a pizza and to return home to await further word on my father.

A few hours later, her home phone rang — it was the call she had been dreading. My mother and I returned to the hospital, where we learned my father had breathed his last. My mother had left instructions that health care personnel were to try to revive him — in the course of that effort, his head had swollen to the point that we would end up having a closed casket for his viewing. With my father disfigured, the finality of his passing seemed all the more somber. My mother tenderly said her goodbyes to him and his body was transported to the funeral home.

Seemingly providentially, when a priest — a man beloved by my parents — celebrated my father's funeral Mass, he focused his homily on the Church's teaching on the resurrection of the dead. He spoke of the beauty of the resurrected body — a concept that gave me great comfort, given how disfigured my father had become in his final moments in the

ICU. I felt God speaking to me through that holy priest, assuring me that the Church's teaching could be trusted.

Perhaps you have experienced the death of someone close to you, and left to wonder about your beloved's ultimate fate. It's important to recognize that God desires the salvation of your loved one more than you do. It can be quite consoling to pray for mercy for your beloved's soul.

You might also consider performing some penitential work on behalf of the Holy Souls in Purgatory, such as cleaning the home or mowing the lawn of an elderly neighbor. Acts of mercy can be tremendously helpful in obtaining graces for those souls who can no longer advocate for themselves.

In hindsight, I can recognize the fact that my father's experience of sickness and death was a blessed time — a time when many blessings poured forth on our family. My father followed his own personal Via Dolorosa — his way of sorrows — in the path to eternal life.

I live in hopeful expectation that I will see my father again — and he will be happier than I had ever known him to be. And his smile will light up the heavens.

Personal Reflections

1. What do you envision a "holy death" to be?
2. To what extent have you struggled with the Church's teaching on life after death?
3. Which deceased friends and/or family members could you pray for today?
4. When have you experienced a Via Dolorosa in your life? What were the blessings hidden within it?

CHAPTER 6
The Ascension from Mary's Perspective

One can imagine that it was a bittersweet time in the Blessed Mother's life. Her beloved Son, Who had overcome death with His glorious Resurrection, was now ascending to the Father. She would no longer see His face or hold His hand. She had lost Him once through His painful death, and now she was losing Him again.

And yet, He was heading to Heaven, body and soul, a feat that had never occurred before. Miraculous and joyous, the Ascension capped off Jesus' remarkable life on earth. He was going to sit at the right hand of the Father to intercede for mankind. For Mary, who had held Jesus in her womb before she cradled Him in her arms, this supernatural event carried particular significance. Her precious Son, on loan to the world, was returning to His Heavenly Father, where He could reign eternally.

Scripture does not say specifically whether Mary was present at the Ascension. However, pious tradition has her there, and in a number of paintings, artists have depicted her at the scene, gazing up at the sky in the company of the Apostles. It only makes sense that the Blessed Mother would be among those gathered for this incredible event. She had accompanied Jesus throughout His life; her devotion knew no bounds. As a mother, she was present at both triumph and tragedy, lending support throughout Christ's life on earth.

Just thinking of the Ascension causes my heart to beat a little faster. What a spectacular moment! I can envision myself among Christ's followers, witnessing this seminal event in the history of the world. We read in the Acts of the Apostles, "as they were looking on, He was lifted up, and a cloud took Him from their sight" (Acts 1:9). How glorious a scene that must have been! Seeing Jesus lifted above the earth and then disappearing into the heavens. It's an occasion that fills me with awe as I recognize the almighty power of God.

And yet, we must also remember the biblical promise that Christ will return to earth again for the Last Judgment.

As the *Catechism of the Catholic Church* states:

> The Last Judgment will come when Christ returns in glory. Only the Father knows the day and the hour; only He determines the moment of its coming. Then through His Son Jesus Christ He will pronounce the final word on all history. We shall know the ultimate meaning of the whole work of

> creation and of the entire economy of salvation and understand the marvelous ways by which His Providence led everything toward its final end. The Last Judgment will reveal that God's justice triumphs over all the injustices committed by His creatures and that God's love is stronger than death (#1040).[11]

When it comes to the Ascension, like the other events in Christ's life, it can be surmised that Mary kept the event in her heart. She would have pondered its meaning, both for herself and for others. She would have demonstrated the quiet acceptance and resignation to God's Holy will that brings peace. As the handmaid of the Lord, Mary would have had the philosophy, "Let it be done, according to God's design."

With Christ's Ascension, our own hopes ascend to Heaven. We know that Jesus is at the right Hand of the Father, eager to hear our prayers. He is also there to prepare a place for us when we complete our earthly journey.

We can also look at the Ascension as foreshadowing Mary's fate. As the sinless vessel through whom Jesus came into the world, she ultimately would be taken up to Heaven as well. The hope that we hold within our own hearts is that we will someday live, body and soul, in Heaven with God, His angels, and His saints.

By imitating the virtues of Mary, and by relying on God's abundant grace, we can someday claim Heaven as our home.

Personal Reflections

1. What comes to your mind when you think about the Ascension?
2. How do you believe Mary viewed the Ascension of her son?
3. Does the Last Judgment fill you with fear or hope? Why is that the case?
4. What things might God be calling you to ponder in your heart this week?

CHAPTER 7
Growing in Virtue: Hope

My mother viewed me as the most hopeful member of our family. I invariably held out hope that something good was around the corner, even when we were in the midst of struggle and strife. At a time when it seemed an impossible dream, I predicted that I would receive a full scholarship to college. Sure enough, it happened, against incredible odds. Turned down for a scholarship to my dream school, I secured an all-tuition-paid financial aid package from our hometown university. While my grade-point average helped to win favor from the financial aid office, I knew I would never have achieved such a feat without the constant help of God.

I distinctly remember a time when my younger sister remarked that, no matter how bad things seemed to get in our family, in the end, everything was fine. There was no doubting that a Supreme Being was watching over us, providing us with tender care. We also had a strong intercessor in the Blessed Mother, who was undoubtedly my mother's favorite saint. My mother taught my sister and me to look to Mary in the gravest of circumstances, knowing that she would intercede for us with her Son.

Hope has a specific definition within the life of the Church. According to the *Catechism*:

> Hope is the theological virtue by which we desire the kingdom of heaven and eternal life as our happiness, placing our trust in Christ's promises and relying not on our own strength, but on the help of the grace of the Holy Spirit. "Let us hold fast the confession of our hope without wavering, for he who promised is faithful." "The Holy Spirit … he poured out upon us richly through Jesus Christ our Savior, so that we might be justified by his grace and become heirs in hope of eternal life" (#1817).

Let's unpack this theologically-rich passage a little bit. The theological virtue of hope aspires to go beyond this world, seeking the eternal bliss which Heaven holds. As we set our sights on Heaven, we realize that we can never achieve such a state of happiness on our own. Rather, it is only through God's grace that we can be united with Him for all time.

Given our sinful state, it would be easy to become discouraged and to think that Heaven is beyond our reach. During difficult times in my life, I have despaired of the possibility of my salvation, thinking (wrongly) that I was beyond the reach of God's merciful love. The fact is, we can easily become discouraged when faced with the reality of our own sinfulness. But we can always have hope in our Redeemer, who loves us beyond all measure and wants to live with us forever in Heaven.

I have found that an antidote to hopelessness is the Sacrament of Reconciliation. It can seem counterintuitive, since in preparing for the Sacrament we must bring to mind all the times we have failed to love God, our neighbors, and ourselves. But the Sacrament provides a healing grace which can bring us immense consolation and peace. We may also find solace in the words of the priest, who counsels us in an effort to help us to avoid such sins in the future.

It is natural to feel some trepidation at the thought of sharing our transgressions in the confessional. It can be helpful to remember that we are confessing our sins before a loving, merciful God who longs for a close relationship with us. And it is such a powerful experience to hear the words, "Your sins are forgiven." Each Confession holds the prospect of a fresh start, an opportunity to conquer our faults and failings and to wipe the slate clean.

When I first returned to the Sacrament of Reconciliation after many years away, I did not hold out much hope of overcoming my sinfulness. Indeed, my most common failures seemed as much a part of my life as my daily habit of brushing my teeth. I thought I just could not let go of certain sins — that they were a part of my DNA.

But in Confession I discovered God's rescue plan for me. Through prayer and penance and the power of His grace, I was able to stop committing some "pet sins." While I must guard against complacency, I recognize that my spiritual muscles have become stronger and I am better-equipped to say "No" to sin.

Hope is not the same thing as presumption — the false idea that we are guaranteed a ticket to Heaven. I recognize that I cannot claim Heaven as my right, but I view it as my goal. I compare it to the basketball game I played in fourth grade (I was not an athlete, and I ended up participating as a team member in only one game). Victory was not guaranteed but, if our team played well, following the instructions of our coach, we had a reasonable chance of success. In the end, though, as in all things, God's providence was at work. None of us could do anything on the court — dribble the ball, pass, or make a basket — without the Lord's help. He was the Master of the court, just as He is the Master of our lives.

Perhaps, though, the best example of hope I can find lies in my memories of my mother's gardens. When I was a little girl, my mother kept a garden along the side of our apartment building and the front of our garage. As my mother weeded and watered, I would stand beside her with my toy watering can, pouring my pretend water into the soil.

Some of the happiest days of my childhood occurred when the first tulips appeared in the spring. It was heavenly, seeing those beautiful pink flowers bursting forth from the ground. In the dead of winter, it was hard to imagine my mother's gardens ever coming to life again. But in April — the month of my parents' wedding anniversary — signs of life would bloom again.

When we feel defeated by sin, it can be difficult to imagine that we will ever reach Heaven. However, just as flowers find life in spring's warmth, so we can find eternal life in the warm embrace of God's love. While it is true that our souls may spend some time in the cleansing state of Purgatory, we can be assured that God wants us to be with Him in Heaven, where the tears of this earthly life are but a memory.

Personal Reflections

1. Would you describe yourself as "hopeful?" Why or why not?
2. What actions can you take to add more hope to your life?
3. Think about the past week and the ways you have fallen short in your walk with God. What particular sins might you work to overcome in the upcoming week?
4. If you frequent the Sacrament of Reconciliation, what do you think keeps you coming back? If it has been a while since your last Confession, what's holding you back?

CHAPTER 8
Saintly Encounters: St. Joseph

As a child, I could not remember a time when he was not there. He was a constant presence, just like my Raggedy Ann doll and the imported doll from Italy that stood watch over my bed. He stood tall on a shelf in the living room, as if he was guarding our apartment against intruders. "He" was a statue of beloved St. Joseph, a humble, holy man who had been adopted as our family's patron saint.

In the bedroom belonging to my mother and father, they kept a holy card featuring a Novena to St. Joseph. As a teenager I prayed it often, but gave up the practice as an adult. However, during the COVID-19 pandemic, my prayer group, which met virtually over Zoom, took up the mantle of St. Joseph and began reciting the prayer of my youth. Even though it had been many years since I had said the prayer, I recognized it as soon as I heard it, since it had been seared into my brain from a young age. It gives me as great a comfort today as it did when I was a child:

> Oh, St. Joseph, whose protection is so great, so strong, so prompt before the

> throne of God, I place in you all my interests and desires. Oh, St. Joseph, do assist me by your powerful intercession, and obtain for me from your divine Son all spiritual blessings, through Jesus Christ, our Lord. So that, having engaged here below your heavenly power, I may offer my thanksgiving and homage to the most loving of fathers. Oh, St. Joseph, I never weary of contemplating you, and Jesus asleep in your arms; I dare not approach while He reposes near your heart. Press Him in my name and kiss His fine head for me and ask Him to return the kiss when I draw my dying breath. St. Joseph, Patron of departing souls — pray for me.[12]

I have always found St. Joseph to be a powerful intercessor. I have asked him to pray to Jesus for everything from a smooth labor and delivery of my beloved baby girl to a successful home sale. I have felt his loving presence during the darkest times of my life, such as the time of the pandemic, when I felt so isolated and frustrated. When I turn to him, I experience his protection and sense that he is near. I find solace in his fatherhood and his wise guidance.

Scripture shows Joseph to be a man of action — but one guided by the inspirations of the Lord. In the gospel of Matthew we read:

> Joseph, her husband, since he was a righteous man, yet unwilling to expose her to shame, decided to divorce her quietly. Such was his intention when, behold, the angel of the Lord appeared to him in a dream and said, "Joseph, son of David, do not be afraid to take Mary your wife into your home. For it is through the Holy Spirit that this child has been conceived in her.
>
> "She will bear a son and you are to name him Jesus, because he will save his people from their sins."
>
> All this took place to fulfill what the Lord had said through the prophet: "Behold, the virgin shall be with child and bear a son, and they shall name him Emmanuel," which means "God is with us."
>
> When Joseph awoke, he did as the angel of the Lord had commanded him and took his wife into his home. He had no relations with her until she bore a son" (Mt 1:19-25).

This scriptural passage demonstrates St. Joseph's receptivity and obedience to the Lord and his respect for and loyalty to his beloved Mary. He could have easily abandoned her in her pregnancy amid the specter of scandal but, instead, he stood by her, offering her support and compassion. He is a model of holiness and purity, providing us with a stellar example of masculine virtue.

In Matthew, we see once again St. Joseph's attentiveness to the Lord's direction:

> When they had departed, behold, the angel of the Lord appeared to Joseph in a dream and said, "Rise, take the child and his mother, flee to Egypt, and stay there until I tell you. Herod is going to search for the child to destroy him."
>
> Joseph rose and took the child and his mother by night and departed for Egypt. He stayed there until the death of Herod, that what the Lord had said through the prophet might be fulfilled, "Out of Egypt I called my son" (Mt 2:13-15).

The foster-father of Jesus consistently looked to the Lord for guidance, relying on a kind of supernatural GPS to direct his steps:

> When Herod had died, behold, the angel of the Lord appeared in a dream to Joseph in Egypt and said, "Rise, take the child and his mother and go to the land of Israel, for those who sought the child's life are dead."
>
> He rose, took the child and his mother, and went to the land of Israel.

> But when he heard that Archelaus was ruling over Judea in place of his father Herod, he was afraid to go back there. And because he had been warned in a dream, he departed for the region of Galilee.
>
> He went and dwelt in a town called Nazareth, so that what had been spoken through the prophets might be fulfilled, "He shall be called a Nazorean" (Mt 2:19-23).

It is no wonder St. Joseph was my family's "go-to guy." Why wouldn't we go to him for help, when all seemed lost? During his life on earth, he proved time and time again to be a man of honor and dependability.

If you are in the midst of a struggle, if you do not know where to turn, consider invoking the aid of St. Joseph. He is a faithful friend who stands ready to assist! We also should keep in mind that, aside from Jesus, there was no one on earth closer to the Blessed Mother than Joseph. If Mary could depend on Joseph in the most trying of times, certainly we can, too.

Personal Reflections

1. When someone mentions St. Joseph to you, what thoughts come to your mind?
2. What impresses you most about St. Joseph's relationship with Mary?
3. Have you ever experienced a dream that you felt held within it a divine command?
4. What prayer petitions do you hold in the silence of your heart that you can bring to St. Joseph today?

CHAPTER 9
Holy Spirit on the Move

I had become quite comfortable with my life. Sure, the recent break-in of my car in my townhouse garage had caused me a bit of worry. And part of my life seemed to be unsettled. I continued to feel my way through the faith of my father and mother, searching for ways to become more committed to Christ. Still, I was generally happy with my work and my living arrangement — especially the fact that I was now so close to my parents and sister that I could walk to their house.

But, seemingly in an instant, circumstances changed. I was scrolling through my emails and saw a job advertised in a nearby state. The position entailed a great deal of writing and communicating with the news media and, as a former journalist, I seemed uniquely qualified for the task.

I applied for the job and was quickly contacted for an interview. I had to drive seven-and-a-half hours to reach my potential employer, but I was up for the trip. After a pleasant round of interviewing, I stopped at a nearby apartment complex to pick up a leasing application, *just in case.*

I was pleasantly surprised when I was offered the job. I hesitated, however. After all, I did like my current job, my townhouse, and my proximity to my family of origin. I decided to let my boss know about the job offer — but also to express to her my doubts.

She got up from her chair and closed the door. She said that she was not going to tell me this — and "this" sounded ominous — but I had sounded as if I was not going to take the new job, so she felt compelled.

"This" was the fact that my current job was being eliminated in a cost-cutting measure. My choice was to take the new job or be unemployed.

The whole situation seemed to give new meaning to the old saying, "Where God closes a door, He opens a window." I needed to climb out the window and head to another state. Alone. Truth be told, a little frightened. With a U-Haul trailer chained to the back of my car.

Sometimes in life, I have found that God gives me a series of "green lights," telling me to move forward. I felt in my heart that this was one of those times. I placed ads in a local newspaper to sell my washer, dryer, and day bed. I was a bit amazed as potential buyers quickly answered the ads and, one by one, my extra possessions left my apartment building.

In a marathon moving session, a few of my co-workers and their children helped me pack up the

U-Haul. We reached the point where we could not fit another single item into it, so we packed the extra goods into our cars and hauled them to my mother's house.

I will never forget the look of pain in my mother's eyes. She was heartbroken that I was moving. I did not want to leave her, my father, or my sister, but I felt God was leading me onto a new path. As much as I loved my mother, I had to obey God's direction.

And so I set out, with my car radio on and my spirits high.

I had just crossed the border between Ohio and Pennsylvania when I heard a strange sound. Suddenly, it became difficult to steer. I pulled over to the side of the highway, shifted the car into park, and carefully exited the vehicle to find out where the trouble was.

I discovered I had a flat tire — on the U-Haul trailer. I was still a number of hours away from my final destination. At this point, I had to make a decision: Should I consider this turn of events to be a bad sign and return to Ohio? Or should I continue on, even though I had no idea what other misadventures might lie ahead?

I called U-Haul and a technician arrived to lend his assistance. I ultimately decided that, having come this far, I did not want to go back to my starting place. Even in the midst of my cross, I felt the Holy

Spirit urging me onward. It was a giant venture into unknown territory as I entrusted the course of my life to Jesus and Mary.

It has now been many years since that fateful trip into the unknown. I have never regretted the move. It brought me independence, new opportunities, and a kick-start to my faith life through the lay Catholic movement known as Cursillo. I now cannot imagine what my life would have been like without the incredible relationships I formed after my leap of faith. I found the old slogan to be true: "You've got a friend in Pennsylvania."

I have to say that I felt a kinship with the Blessed Virgin Mary in my travels. Scripture shows us how Mary traveled to Bethlehem, to Egypt, and to Nazareth, fulfilling God's will each time. She trusted in the Lord to see her through challenging journeys and difficult circumstances, relying not on her own understanding, but on the wisdom of the Almighty.

Perhaps you, too, are receiving promptings from God to ease out of your comfort zone and forge a new path. The Lord may be leading you to a new job, a new home, a new relationship, a new ministry, or a new hobby. Why not spend some quiet time with your Creator and contemplate the possibilities that are before you? You may be surprised by what the Lord has to say!

Personal Reflections

1. In what ways is God calling you to something "new?"
2. How can you imitate Mary's trust in the Lord this week?
3. What are the "flat tires" that you are encountering in your life right now?
4. Looking back, how has God steered your earthly journey in new directions?

CHAPTER 10

Descent of the Holy Spirit Upon the Apostles

I have often wondered what it would have been like to have been one of the Apostles in the wake of Christ's Ascension into Heaven. I cannot help but think that those men closest to Jesus would have keenly felt His absence on planet Earth. A longing must have risen in their hearts for a reunion with their Lord, Who had given them so much while He was with them.

How much more so was the pain of the Blessed Mother, who no longer saw her Son's precious face. Mary endured the separation from her beloved Jesus with incomparable dignity and grace, and pondered the amazing turn of events in the silence of her heart. Indeed, Mary is the ultimate role model for all of those mothers who struggle with the loss of a child.

God did not abandon Mary and the Apostles. He sent His Holy Spirit to them in a breathtakingly beautiful way at Pentecost. In the Acts of the Apostles, we read about the arrival of the Third Person of the Holy Trinity:

> When the time for Pentecost was fulfilled, they were all in one place together. And

> suddenly there came from the sky a noise like a strong driving wind, and it filled the entire house in which they were. Then there appeared to them tongues as of fire, which parted and came to rest on each of them. And they were all filled with the Holy Spirit and began to speak in different tongues, as the Spirit enabled them to proclaim (Acts 2:1-4).

The arrival of the Holy Spirit marked the birth of the Church. He gave the Apostles the wisdom and courage they needed to spread the Gospel throughout the land. With the ability to speak in different languages, they were now able to communicate the message of Christ to people who may never have met Him while He was on earth.

I will never forget the day that I received an outpouring of the Holy Spirit through my Confirmation. It just so happened that that was also the day of a state-wide test for high school students who were competing to demonstrate their proficiency in the Spanish language. I went to the testing center, took the exam, quickly changed into my ivory Confirmation dress, and raced to the church in time to receive the Sacrament.

I had chosen as my Confirmation name "Dominique," and adopted St. Dominic as my patron. I wish I could say that the illustrious accomplishments of St. Dominic had inspired my decision, but, in all honesty, I selected the name because it appeared in a favorite book of mine called *The Court of the Stone Children*. The book told the story of a girl who befriended a mysterious child, Dominique, in a French museum. I found the plot so captivating, and Dominique so enchanting, that it made a life-long impression on me.

Like many of my generation, I did not understand the significance of my Confirmation at the time that I received the Sacrament. I realized that it was a special occasion, topped off with lunch at a favorite restaurant with my Confirmation sponsor and my family. There was ceremonial picture-taking and congratulations all around. But somehow I had failed to realize the importance of the outpouring of the Holy Spirit upon me. I was caught up in worldly pursuits, and I ended up spending more than a decade in a kind of spiritual wilderness.

But the spark that had been left in my soul at my Confirmation was still there and, eventually, it grew into a flame which continues to light my path to this day.

Many years after my Confirmation, I recognized the significance of St. Dominic in my life. A renowned preacher, he inspired me to give talks on the sanctity of human life. I felt a kinship to him as I tried to persuade audiences of the dignity and value of each person, from the moment of conception to the instant of natural death. In St. Dominic, I had found a role model who could help me achieve oratorical successes that I could not accomplish on my own.

I now have a habit of invoking the Holy Spirit at the start of my day. It is comforting to know that He is with me, ready to inspire. While I cannot claim to follow His direction perfectly, I have noticed that I am becoming better able to understand and heed His inspirations.

I have to say that there are times that I brush off the promptings of the Holy Spirit. Like the time my Aunt Mary warned me to be sure to empty my car of various belongings before I headed into my apartment for the night. I ignored her advice and, lo and behold, the next day I discovered someone had broken into my car — the aforementioned break-in. The shattered glass from my broken car window proved to be a vivid reminder that I need to be more attuned to the Lord's direction.

Perhaps, like me, you find yourself struggling to hear the whispers of the Holy Spirit. I urge you to keep trying. It can be challenging to find the Holy Spirit's voice, but He is always there to offer assistance, if only we heed His warnings.

I encourage you to be like Mary and the Apostles and invoke the Holy Spirit on a regular basis. You may be surprised at how the Third Person of the

Holy Trinity works in your mind and heart, leading you to new adventures and incredible destinations!

Personal Reflections

1. When you were confirmed, you received a sacramental strengthening of the gift of the Holy Spirit in your heart. Did you cooperate with that special gift in the months and years after your Confirmation? Did you experience any fruit from that gift in your life?
2. If you have not been confirmed, what would it take for you to enter RCIA (the Rite of Christian Initiation of Adults) to prepare for your Confirmation?
3. Looking back on the past week, can you identify any instances where the Holy Spirit was at work?
4. What challenges in your life can you give over to the Holy Spirit today?

CHAPTER 11
Growing in Virtue: Love of God

I remember, as an elementary school student, drinking in the words of my teacher as she offered the religious lesson of the day. I was attending a Catholic school, and religion was an essential part of the curriculum. I don't know why — maybe it was the lovely weather, or a treat I had recently received — but in that moment, I felt a profound love of God.

I was fortunate, because I was being raised in a home with a father who truly modeled God's love. My Daddy was gentle and kind and was always so encouraging to my sister and me. When I had misbehaved as a toddler, he had spanked me once — and afterward vowed never to do so again. As a result, I had zero fear of my father. I knew he loved me deeply and I could rest confidently in that love. I always knew my father treasured me and did not want anything bad to happen to me.

Unfortunately, when I became an adult, my view of God shifted. I saw Him as the Enforcer, demanding obedience and poised to punish me swiftly and unmercifully if I wandered off the path of righteousness. I falsely thought that He was eager to remind me of my sins and that my least transgression would lead to disaster.

These thoughts did not come out of nowhere. I was in an abusive relationship and I viewed the individual who was abusing me as all-powerful, like a god. The toxic environment in which I was then living filled me with a constant state of dread and a fear of the future. I felt a sense of hopelessness that emotionally paralyzed me and led me to the brink of despair.

I believe it was the prayers of my mother that eventually led me out of that dark chapter of my life. Free of the abuse, I began to rediscover the faith of my youth. And, in that quest for knowledge, I found a God who was just, yes, but also all-merciful. This was a God who loved me beyond all reason, who was ready and eager to embrace His prodigal daughter and gently lead her to a place of peace.

Today I most keenly feel the love of God in the Eucharist. The idea of Jesus giving to me His Body and Blood under the appearances of bread and wine is just incredible. I come to Holy Communion eager to unite with Him. The Eucharist has become for me a soul-stirring experience and one I long for each week. I would say those moments right after receiving Holy Communion are an amazing opportunity to share in the goodness of God.

I am also enamored by adoration of the Blessed Sacrament. During my Holy Hour each week, I give over to Jesus, through the hands of Mary, whatever trials and travails I am facing. I know that the Lord hears me, and I am often amazed at how He resolves my difficulties.

My love for the Lord also grows through each Confession. I am overwhelmed by the idea that God freely forgives my sins and that He stands ever ready to repair a relationship broken by sin. I relish the grace of the Sacrament and have found that, over time, Reconciliation has helped me to put to bed some of the pesky sins in my life. But I also understand that I am a work in progress and not sin-free. That simple and humble fact just makes me love God all the more.

I have also found my love of God growing as a result of prayer. I have a regular morning routine in which I recite the Divine Mercy Chaplet and the Holy Rosary, along with praying a special extra decade of the Rosary for the conversion of those who work in opposition to the protection of innocent human life. During the course of the day, I engage in a Spiritual Communion where I ask Jesus into my heart.

Meanwhile, in the evening, I pray in gratitude for the many blessings of the day … consider the times when I was the best version of myself and the worst version of myself … and ask for forgiveness and peace. I recently added Night Prayer to my routine, using the Catholic phone app known as Hallow. This special time of communicating with God has greatly enhanced my spiritual life and my love of Him.

I must admit I still struggle with recognizing the voice of God in my life. That is why I often pray for the Holy Spirit to enlighten my mind and soften my heart. Perhaps it is the writer in me, but my mind is often cluttered with my own thoughts and words. It takes a great deal of discipline for me to "turn down the volume" and to listen to the Lord. But I am working on it, and I find the more that I quiet my mind, the more I open myself up to the love of the Almighty.

Mary serves as a model for devotion to God. She was willing to give up her own preferences and plans to live out God's call as the mother of Jesus. In her Magnificat (Lk 1:46-55), we find a tremendous love for the Lord and a beautiful reflection of the tenderness and compassion of God:

> My soul proclaims the greatness of the Lord; my spirit rejoices in God my savior. For he has looked upon his handmaid's lowliness; behold, from now on will all ages call me blessed. The Mighty One has done great things for me, and holy is his name, his mercy is from age to age to those who fear him. He has shown might with his arm, dispersed the arrogant of mind and heart. He has thrown down the

> rulers from their thrones but lifted up the lowly. The hungry he has filled with good things; the rich he has sent away empty. He has helped Israel his servant, remembering his mercy, according to his promise to our fathers, to Abraham and to his descendants forever.

The Magnificat is such a profound outpouring of love for the Lord. Mary recognizes the greatness of God and the astounding impact He has on her daily life. She exposes her own vulnerability, noting her lowliness. Yet she also sees the blessings that have flowed throughout her days. Her eloquence is so touching and so meaningful for those of us who long for a greater intimacy with the Almighty.

My prayer for you is that you feel God's love in a fantastic, life-altering way this week, and that you will be inspired to share that love with others.

Personal Reflections:

1. What is your current view of God, and how has your perception changed over the years?
2. In what ways can you grow this week in the love of God?
3. Can you remember a time in which you experienced the love of God in a profound way?
4. What strikes you most about Mary's Magnificat and how can you apply that passage to your daily life?

CHAPTER 12
Saintly Encounter: St. Paul

As a child, I held a certain fascination for St. Paul. After all, he wrote world-renowned letters, took part in incredible adventures, and preached to people who desperately needed to hear the good news of Christ. I considered him a sort of Superman of Scripture, possessing otherworldly persuasive skills. I was, quite rightly, in awe of him and the masterful way he could share Christ's teachings.

Of course, Paul was not always the saintly figure we admire today. Prior to his conversion, living as Saul, he was quite the scoundrel, routinely persecuting Christians. But on the road to Damascus, a light flashed, he fell to the ground, and he heard a greeting that would change the course of his life — along with the many converts he ultimately would attract to the Christian faith.

In Acts 9:4-5, we read that a voice called out to him, saying:

> "Saul, Saul, why are you persecuting me?" He said, "Who are you sir?" The reply came, "I am Jesus, whom you are persecuting."

Jesus then instructed him to go into the city, where he would be told what to do.

But Saul faced a challenge — he was now blind. Thankfully, prompted by God, a man named Ananias came to his rescue:

> Ananias went and entered the house; laying his hands on him, he said, "Saul, my brother, the Lord has sent me, Jesus who appeared to you on the way by which you came, that you may regain your sight and be filled with the Holy Spirit."
>
> Immediately things like scales fell from his eyes and he regained his sight. He got up and was baptized, and when he had eaten, he recovered his strength (Acts 9:17-19).

Following his dramatic conversion, St. Paul was like Mary in his steadfast devotion to Christ. Time and time again, he demonstrated a heroic love of God which, in turn, drew many souls into the Christian faith.

Each time I read St. Paul's second letter to the Corinthians, I am awed by his dedication to Jesus, even in the midst of terrible trials. Here the apostle describes the terrors that he faced in his journey with God:

> Three times I was beaten with rods, once I was stoned, three times I was shipwrecked,

> I passed a night and a day on the deep; on frequent journeys, in danger from rivers, dangers from robbers, dangers from my own race, dangers from Gentiles, dangers in the city, danger in the wilderness, dangers at sea, dangers among false brothers; in toil and hardship, through many sleepless nights, through hunger and thirst, through frequent fastings, through cold and exposure.
>
> And apart from these things, there is the daily pressure upon me of my anxiety for all the churches. Who is weak, and I am not weak? Who is led to sin, and I am not indignant?
>
> If I must boast, I will boast of the things that show my weakness (2 Cor 11:25-30).

Reading St. Paul's account of his sufferings, I am amazed by his resilience and dedication to the Gospel. And I have to ask myself, "Am I similarly willing to risk everything for the sake of Jesus and His teaching?"

In St. Paul I find a tremendous role model for my own faith journey. While I may never be shipwrecked, I have my own share of toils and sleepless nights. I can turn to St. Paul for intercession with the Father as I face my own set of troubles.

Saint Paul also happens to be the patron saint of the worldwide Cursillo movement, which has brought me closer to Christ with its spiritual tripod of piety, study, and apostolic action. By following a daily schedule of prayer, spiritual reading, and kindnesses toward my neighbor, I have seen little miracles happen in my life. I wish the same for you!

Personal Reflections

1. As Christians, we are called to constant conversion. What conversions of heart have you experienced in your life?
2. How can you model St. Paul and the Blessed Mother this week in your love of God?
3. What sacrifices have you made to draw closer to Christ?
4. How can you share the good news of Christ with others today?

CHAPTER 13
A Heavenly Experience

I wholeheartedly believe that, every so often in this life, we experience a taste of Heaven — as delicious as any of the cakes prepared with love and affection by your mother, grandmother, or someone else close to you. It is in these moments when we feel God's tenderness in a deep and profound way. It is as if He has stopped whatever He was doing as Master of the Universe, placed His attention squarely on us, and enwrapped us in a big bear hug.

At these times, there seems to be no escaping His love — nor do we want to. We just wish the moment could last forever.

I will never know what it was like for the Blessed Mother to be assumed into Heaven. She was sinless, and I spend my evenings asking for forgiveness from the Almighty for my seemingly endless list of sins. She bore the Savior of the world and humbly accepted her role as Mother of God.

Without Mary, Heaven's gates would have been closed to me and the other residents of planet Earth. However, during those precious instances when I am savoring life, I would like to think that I have an inkling of what it must be like to experience God in His Heavenly realm — the beatific vision that I long to see.

These foretastes of Heaven remind me of Easter Sunday when, following the sacrifices and sufferings of Lent and Good Friday, we experience the miracle of the Resurrection.

My mother was an expert at celebrating Easter. It was a grand affair, filled with carnation corsages, baskets brimming with candy and assorted trinkets, and specially-selected ensembles with party dresses and matching spring coats. Inspired by my mother, to this day I try to celebrate Easter in style, knowing that I am carrying on a beloved family tradition.

Before I describe a major heavenly experience in my life, I have to talk about the years I spent in a kind of wilderness, waiting for an affirmative answer to my prayer. The prayer was borne out of an intense heartache caused by a painful episode in my motherhood.

Following my divorce, I had been undergoing child custody proceedings when my daughter's father took her to Canada. Since he had transported her out of the country without notifying the court, the judge awarded me legal custody of her. I was to pick her up at a halfway point between my home and the place where she was staying in Canada.

But when I arrived at the destination, she and her father were nowhere to be found.

Not long after, my beloved father died in Ohio. My attorney spoke with the attorney representing my daughter's father, and they agreed that my daughter should be present at the funeral. Under our agreement, her father would accompany her there, then, after the funeral was over, she would return home with me.

But my grief over my father's death was compounded by the fact that, once again, Gabriella did not appear.

One January day when I was on board a bus heading to Washington, D.C., I received a call from my office. A co-worker said that I needed to contact my seven-year-old daughter's school principal in Canada right away. I immediately phoned the principal, who told me that he believed my little girl had been taken to the Middle East by her father. This turn of events came as a complete shock, and, after ending the phone call, I literally cried out in pain. I had experienced divorce and had undergone child custody proceedings, but this was the most painful blow of all.

My contact with my daughter became limited to cyberspace and was quite sporadic. Every so often I would talk to her via Skype or Facebook Messenger. Not being able to give her a hug was perhaps the greatest cross of all.

I clung to Jesus with a fierce grip, for I knew that, without Him, I would fall apart. He had also given me a wonderful group of friends who stood by me in the darkest of times. I drew from their strength when I thought I had none of my own left to rely on.

I explored every legal option to try to get my daughter back. I kept thinking that she belonged in the U.S. and that she needed to come home — immediately. But, seemingly at every turn, my hope for her swift return flickered and then flamed out. The U.S. has no extradition treaty with the country where her father took her. I kept a journal of every phone call I made and each e-mail I sent to try to secure her safe journey back to the U.S. The journal ultimately numbered more than 400 pages.

I prayed Rosaries, Divine Mercy Chaplets, and Novenas to ask God for her return. At Mass and at Adoration, I dedicated my time before the Blessed Sacrament to the cause of being reunited with her. The answer from the Lord always seemed to be, "No."

The years passed, a decade and more. Then, one glorious summer day, my daughter texted me. She wanted to attend a beloved cousin's wedding, and thought she could visit me afterward. It had been 16 years since I had seen her in person. My little girl was now a lovely young woman, an accomplished writer and ballerina, whose eloquence with words and with motion astounded me. True, I had only seen her dance in online videos, but I could tell that she possessed a rare talent which was simply incredible.

We faced a hurdle, however — the plane ticket. She could not afford it, and neither could I. But, out of the blue, a friend offered to pay for her travel — more evidence of God's amazing providence.

Even after my daughter had her plane ticket, I still wondered whether I would actually end up seeing her. I had had 16 years of disappointments, and I did not know how I would handle another one.

Still, I held out hope that, finally, my dream would come true.

And on a chilly September day, it did.

We had decided to meet at a hotel about two hours away from my home. I enlisted the aid of a friend, who agreed to accompany me to offer moral support. We arrived early and sat down in the hotel lobby, our hearts filled with anticipation. My eyes were trained on the elevator, thinking that she would be coming down from her room. But what I did not realize is that she was having brunch with some of the members of the wedding party before meeting me.

And so, after a few minutes of waiting, I noticed a blonde-haired, graceful young woman exiting the hotel restaurant. While I had not seen my daughter in person since she was an elementary school student, I knew instantly that the young woman walking toward me was my cherished child. She smiled and we began to engage in conversation as if no time had elapsed since our last meeting.

We — my daughter, my friend, and I — left the hotel to go exploring. At one point during the weekend, we stopped to snap a photo at a quaint location which had been decorated for Halloween. In the picture — which is now my computer screensaver — you see my daughter, a scarecrow, and me, sitting beside a plethora of pumpkins.

In the moment when my friend took the picture, I thought to myself, "If only during those 16 years when I was waiting to see my daughter, I had known one lovely day I would be sitting next to her in a pumpkin patch, I never would have worried."

Personal Reflections

1. When was the last time you experienced what you considered to be a foretaste of Heaven?
2. In what ways has the past week provided you with heavenly experiences?
3. Have you ever prayed for years for a particular gift? If so, what gift have you found in the period of waiting?
4. Have you ever longed to be reunited with someone? How did you experience God in that longing?

CHAPTER 14
The Assumption of the Blessed Mother

It is to me one of those jaw-dropping mysteries of the Holy Rosary: the Assumption of the Blessed Mother into Heaven. I wish I had been present to witness this phenomenal event, which is a testament to Mary's fidelity to the Lord and the immaculate state of her heart. Conceived without sin and sinless throughout her amazing life, Mary held and continues to hold a special place in the life of the Church. As it states in the *Catechism of the Catholic Church*:

> Finally, the Immaculate Virgin, preserved free from all stain of original sin, when the course of her earthly life was finished, was taken up body and soul into heavenly glory, and exalted by the Lord as Queen over all things, so that she might be the more fully conformed to her Son, the Lord of lords and conqueror of sin and death (#966).

It is important to note that, while Mary certainly was like us in many respects, her sinlessness set her apart. So it makes sense that she would leave this earth in a most spectacular way.

Imagine the scene as Mary is assumed body and soul into Heaven — how utterly magnificent and so in keeping with her role as Mediatrix, forming a bridge between God and man. Mary's glorious Assumption offers a significant connection to Christ's Resurrection, as the *Catechism* further states:

> The Assumption of the Blessed Virgin is a singular participation in her Son's Resurrection and an anticipation of the resurrection of other Christians (#966).

Mary gives us hope that we, too, can someday live, body and soul, in Heaven, sharing in the endless happiness of the Lord. Jesus, through His sacrificial death and incredible Resurrection, opened up the gates of Heaven for us, so that we could live with Him and His mother forever. It is so comforting to know that Mary, as mother of us all, seeks to assist us from her dwelling place in Heaven. As noted in the *Catechism*, the Byzantine Liturgy articulates Mary's role in the most eloquent way:

> In giving birth you kept your virginity; in your Dormition you did not leave the world, O Mother of God, but were joined to the source of Life. You conceived the living God and, by your prayers, will deliver our souls from death.[13]

Venerable Pope Pius XII defined the dogma of the Assumption on November 1, 1950, in an apostolic constitution known as *Munificentissimus Deus* ("The most bountiful God").[14] In this document, the Holy Father notes that St. Alphonsus once wrote that "Jesus did not wish to have the body of Mary corrupted after death, since it would have been redounded to his own dishonor to have her virginal flesh, from which he himself had assumed flesh, reduced to dust."[15]

The Assumption further demonstrates Mary's role as the "new Eve," heralding in a new era in which the Lord saves His people and opens for them the realm of Heaven. As Pope Pius XII stated:

> We must remember especially that, since the second century, the Virgin Mary has been designated by the holy Fathers as the new Eve, who, although subject to the new Adam, is most intimately associated with him in that struggle against the infernal foe which, as foretold in the protoevangelium, would finally result in that most complete victory over the sin and death which are always mentioned together in the writings of the Apostle of the Gentiles. Consequently, just as the glorious resurrection of Christ was an essential part and the final sign of this victory, so that struggle which was common to the Blessed Virgin

> and her divine Son should be brought to a close by the glorification of her body, for the same Apostle says: "When this mortal thing hath put on immortality, then shall come to pass the saying that is written: Death is swallowed up in victory."[16]

The Assumption demonstrates Mary's victorious conquest, her crushing of the very serpent who tempted the first Eve. Through Mary, humanity experiences a kind of rebirth which carries with it great hope. As a result, we can look to Mary to help us, through our prayers, to touch the heart of God.

Personal Reflections

1. Spend a few minutes contemplating the Assumption of Mary. What thoughts and feelings come to you?
2. In what ways does the Assumption give you hope?
3. What link can you see between the Assumption of Mary and the Resurrection of Jesus?
4. Take a few minutes to tell Mary what is in your heart this week and ask her to intercede for you with Jesus.

CHAPTER 15
Growing in Virtue: Devotion to Our Lady

When I was a little girl, I was a bit confused about the role of Mary in the life of the Church. After all, so many titles had been attributed to her, from Our Lady of Guadalupe to Our Lady of Lourdes. The proliferation of names confused me, as did her designation of Mother of God. If God existed for all time, how could He have a mother? How could a mere human creature assume such a lofty status?

To me, it all defied common sense and, as a six-year-old, I was all about common sense.

As I matured, I recognized that Mary was, herself, something of a mystery. She was a virgin who gave birth — a woman who was conceived without sin and who lived a blameless life. She was so unlike me, and yet we were both human beings beloved by God.

As a working journalist, I thought myself too busy for religious devotions, other than Mass. Stories proliferated every day — stories I had to cover in-depth for what my co-workers and I called long-form radio reports. I fully believed that I, as a journalist, was only as good as my last story — therefore, each news report had to be exceptional. In addition, I was vying constantly for the next big journalism award, the one which would establish me as a standout among my peers.

Over time, as I collected what I called my "hardware" (journalism awards), I came to the conclusion that no single award would bring me lasting happiness, and no one story would redeem me. My life had become disordered, as my journalism career became my "god." I realized I needed to shift my perspective, to honor God as "Number One" in my daily schedule.

Mary offered me an inviting pathway to God. I felt comfortable going to her with my intentions — intentions which she could share with our Heavenly Father. I would go to a statue of her outside of my parish church and offer my most fervent desire for her to pass along to the Lord.

I renewed my daily Rosary, sensing it was vital for helping me to establish a link with both Mary and God. In meditating on the mysteries, I grew closer to the woman who had been named Mother of all the Living. I did not regard her as a goddess, but as a trusted ally. I instinctively knew that she would listen to each prayer and treasure it in the confines of her heart.

One devotion that has become quite important to me is the Our Lady of Mt. Carmel Novena.[17] Over the course of nine days, I reach out to Mary — the "beautiful Flower of Carmel" — and ask for her assistance. A cherished friend of mine was praying the Novena when she made her Cursillo weekend — a weekend which drew her even closer to Mary and her Son Jesus. I have brought many intentions to Our Lady through this powerful Novena, and plan to continue to do so in the future.

Litanies are another way to foster devotion to Mary. According to the global Catholic broadcasting network EWTN, a litany is a prayer form which includes a number of different petitions and a series of fixed responses such as "Lord have mercy."[18] Litanies date back to the fourth century and have a role to play in the Church's liturgy.[19]

One of my personal favorite private litanies is the Litany of the Blessed Virgin:[20]

Lord have mercy on us, *Christ have mercy on us*
Lord have mercy on us.
Christ, hear us, *Christ graciously hear us*

God the father of Heaven, *have mercy on us*
God, the Son, Redeemer of the World, *have mercy on us*
God the Holy Spirit, *have mercy on us*
Holy Trinity, one God, *have mercy on us*

Holy Mary, *pray for us*
Holy Mother of God, *pray for us*
Holy Virgin of virgins, *pray for us*
Mother of Christ, *pray for us*

Mother of Divine Grace, *pray for us*
Mother most pure, *pray for us*
Mother most chaste, *pray for us*
Mother inviolate, *pray for us*
Mother undefiled, *pray for us*
Mother most amiable, *pray for us*
Mother most admirable, *pray for us*
Mother of good counsel, *pray for us*
Mother of our Creator, *pray for us*
Mother of our Savior, *pray for us*
Virgin most prudent, *pray for us*
Virgin most venerable, *pray for us*
Virgin most renowned, *pray for us*
Virgin most powerful, *pray for us*
Virgin most merciful, *pray for us*
Virgin most faithful, *pray for us*
Mirror of justice, *pray for us*
Seat of wisdom, *pray for us*
Cause of our joy, *pray for us*
Spiritual vessel, *pray for us*
Vessel of honor, *pray for us*
Singular vessel of devotion, *pray for us*
Mystical rose, *pray for us*
Tower of David, *pray for us*
Tower of ivory, *pray for us*
House of gold, *pray for us*
Ark of the covenant, *pray for us*
Gate of Heaven, *pray for us*
Morning star, *pray for us*
Health of the sick, *pray for us*
Refuge of sinners, *pray for us*

Comforter of the afflicted, *pray for us*
Help of Christians, *pray for us*
Queen of Angels, *pray for us*
Queen of Patriarchs, *pray for us*
Queen of Prophets, *pray for us*
Queen of Apostles, *pray for us*
Queen of Martyrs, *pray for us*
Queen of Confessors, *pray for us*
Queen of Virgins, *pray for us*
Queen of all Saints, *pray for us*
Queen conceived without original sin, *pray for us*
Queen assumed into Heaven, *pray for us*
Queen of the most holy Rosary, *pray for us*
Queen of Peace, *pray for us*

Lamb of God, Who takes away the sins of the world, *spare us, O Lord*

Lamb of God, Who takes away the sins of the world, *graciously hear us, O Lord*

Lamb of God, Who takes away the sins of the world, *have mercy on us.*

Grant, we beseech Thee, O Lord, God, that we, Thy servants, may enjoy perpetual health of mind and body, and by the glorious intercession of the Blessed Mary, ever Virgin, be delivered from present sorrow and enjoy eternal gladness. Through Christ, our Lord. Amen.

We can also grow in our devotion to our Lady through meditations, especially by meditating on the mysteries of the Holy Rosary. One often overlooked aspect of fulfilling the First Saturday devotions is meditating for 15 minutes on a Rosary mystery. The Fourth Glorious Mystery, the Assumption, is an excellent mystery to reflect upon in order to expand our love of Mary. To ponder the instance when she is taken body and soul into Heaven is to enter into a sublime mystery with her — to join in her joy. It is comforting to know that she has taken her place in Heaven where she can intercede day and night for us as we make our way through a valley of tears.

Personal Reflections

1. What are some of your favorite devotions to Mary?
2. What are some new devotions that you could incorporate into your day?
3. Since beginning this book, have you noted a growth in your love of the Blessed Mother?
4. Which special intention can you place in Mary's hands today?

CHAPTER 16
Saintly Encounter: St. Monica

When I think of St. Monica, I cannot help but feel sympathy toward her. Her wayward son had ignored her pleas to embrace Christ and His Cross, causing her to spend years praying for Augustine's salvation. As the mother of a prodigal, she must have experienced frustration and a sizeable amount of emotional pain. To have the gift of faith and to see a loved one abandon the path of virtue is a special hardship.

No prayer is ever in vain, and certainly Monica's years of beseeching our Lord led to good fruit. Her son eventually had his "come to Jesus" moment, left his sinful ways behind, and became a giant of the Catholic faith, a Doctor of the Church. Monica's story serves as an inspiration to so many mothers who are concerned about the spiritual health of their offspring. In the ever-faithful Monica, they find a kindred spirit — and a holy woman deserving of emulation.

I meet so many, many mothers and fathers who are despondent over their adult children's rejection of the faith. These were parents who gave good example, prayed fervently, and took their young children to Mass each Sunday. And yet, their children ultimately have chosen a different path — a path away from their parents' religious practices. Such stories are heartbreaking, and demonstrate the powerful pull of the secular culture in which we live. And yet, I strongly believe that we can discover hope and inspiration in St. Monica's holy example in the midst of similar trials.

In the accounts I have read of the life of St. Monica, I have discovered that she actually had much in common with the Blessed Mother. Like Mary, she took her motherhood quite seriously. And also like Mary, she had a son for whom she would readily suffer and sacrifice. Ultimately, both Mary and Monica were mothers whose children would lead others to the Heavenly Father. Both women offer portraits of perseverance in the face of great obstacles.

Therefore, in studying the life of Monica, we can find ourselves drawing closer to the Blessed Mother. Monica, in essence, provides a gateway to Mary and to her abiding love for us all. Both are special patrons of mothers, and can therefore light the way for those who see their children struggling in darkness.

Saint Monica knows the particular struggles of single mothers, having been left to raise three children on her own following her husband's death.[21] Born in the fourth century, this valiant woman of faith was dedicated to Christianity. But her son

Augustine was not, causing her to drop to her knees in humble prayer for his eternal soul. A priest once remarked that it was "not possible that the son of so many tears should perish."[22]

God was, indeed, faithful to Monica, delivering her son from a spiritual abyss. He became a gifted philosopher and brilliant bishop, leaving behind a life of sinful pursuits. Augustine credited his mother with serving as the source of his Christian faith. Monica lived to see Augustine baptized, but died shortly thereafter in 387 A.D.

Pope Benedict XVI recognized the connection between Monica and Mary:

> St. Monica and St. Augustine invite us to turn confidently to Mary, Seat of Wisdom. Let us entrust Christian parents to her so that, like Monica, they may accompany their children's progress with their own example and prayers. Let us commend youth to the Virgin Mother of God so that, like Augustine, they may always strive for the fullness of Truth and Love which is Christ: He alone can satisfy the deepest desires of the human heart.[23]

I believe that it is also important to note that St. Monica is a patron saint for survivors of abuse. Her husband, Patricius, was known for his violent temper. Sadly, so many of us have experienced the ravages of abuse — be it physical, emotional, sexual, psychological, or even spiritual. In our suffering, we can turn to Monica for her intercession for our healing.

I used to think healing from abuse was just a pipe dream. The trauma was so overwhelming, I could not even imagine escaping from it. However, by working with trained healthcare professionals and devoting much energy to prayer, I have discovered that glorious place of hope and healing. It is there that I feel the wonderful power of God.

If you or someone you love is a survivor of abuse, please know that I am praying that a path to healing will appear. Connecting with an organization such as Catholic Charities USA® (catholiccharitiesusa.org) can be a source of strength and support for you.

In addition, the Grief to Grace program offers retreats which address the psychological and emotional needs of abuse survivors. I attended the program and experienced the healing touch of Christ through this innovative, holistic approach to ministering to the wounds of abuse. You can learn more at grief-to-grace-lsi.squarespace.com.

Personal Reflections

1. What are your initial impressions of St. Monica?
2. What parallels can you draw between Monica and the Blessed Mother?
3. What special intentions can you take to Monica now?
4. What's stopping you from reaching a glorious place of healing and hope?

CHAPTER 17
Accepting the Queenship of Motherhood

While it was never explicitly stated, my mother was definitely Queen of our home. My father often referred to her as the most beautiful woman in the world and, as a child, I had no reason to doubt him. In appearance, she favored the movie star Elizabeth Taylor, and I thought her to be quite glamorous with her impeccable hair and her wide, engaging smile. She was definitely one to light up a room as soon as she entered it, and I was in awe of her.

If home life were a show, my mother was definitely the star of it. She was not a prima donna, but she was a force to be reckoned with. I cannot imagine my father trying to make a major decision without her input. While she could be reticent in public, she had a strong voice in private and did not hesitate to make her feelings known.

But what made my mother truly beautiful was her service to others. She was the consummate volunteer and gave of her time and talent quite freely. She readily agreed to be a "room mother" to my class at school — a task which involved seemingly endless rounds of baking cupcakes and managing juice spills.

When I was struck by an older student on the playground, my mother came to my rescue by serving as a playground monitor, keeping not only me but the rest of my schoolmates safe. She was a vocal member of the Parent Teacher Association and even volunteered to serve on a committee to launch a new school.

My mother also quietly volunteered to perform tasks that others simply did not want to do. For instance, she agreed to teach her brother-in-law to drive when no one else was willing to step in and help. If she saw a need, she quickly went about the business of filling it. In advance of her wedding, she lobbied the parish to install a handrail so that her older guests would have an easier time making it up the steps of the church.

In her time on earth, my mother Anne lived out the queenship of motherhood, imitating her saintly model, the Blessed Mother. She saw her primary vocation in life as mother and, even though motherhood materialized for her relatively late in life, she pursued her vocation with a passion. I always knew that my mother fiercely loved my sister and me, and that she would do anything in her power to make our lives better. She saw children as a gift and, while she longed for more, she realized that she was richly blessed by the presence of her two girls.

Far too often in our 21st century world, mothers are not treated as queens. The abortion industry robs women of their motherhood, leaving them to grieve the loss of their children. Mothers often lack sufficient material and emotional resources, increasing the threat of depression and other psychological disturbances. Women are often the victims in domestic violence situations, which pose a threat not only to their physical well-being but also to their emotional state. It is difficult to serve as queen of the castle when your home is wracked by unrest.

This is why it is so important for us to work to instill self-respect in our girls. With a healthy self-image, girls can gain the confidence necessary to be successful mothers. It is also important to point out that all women are called to be spiritual mothers, offering tender care to the souls in their midst. This concept should be taught to girls at a young age so that they have a better understanding of their place in the world.

It is also critical for us to appeal to Mary to help us reverence mothers in our homes and in our society at large. Their role in sustaining life — both physical and spiritual — is unparalleled, despite the claims made by those who falsely assert that mothers are no longer necessary.

To recognize the queenship of mothers is not to denigrate fathers; rather, it is simply an acceptance of the truth of the manner in which women were designed to function in society.

Mother's Day should not be relegated to one holiday in May. Instead, we should pay respect to mothers every day. Whether it is offering to babysit for an overwhelmed mother of young ones or taking an older mother to the grocery store, we can do much to celebrate the mothers in our midst.

Personal Reflections

1. What was your relationship like with your mother? Consider taking the topic to prayer.
2. If you are female, what are you doing to serve out your spiritual motherhood?
3. If you are male, how can you honor the mothers in your life?
4. What tangible thing can you do this week to help a mother in need?

CHAPTER 18
The Coronation of Mary as Queen of Heaven and Earth

Perhaps the most glorious encounter we can have with Mary is by reflecting on her title as Queen of Heaven and Earth. She is a unique figure in that she is royalty, yet she is also just a prayer away.

As it states in the *Catechism of the Catholic Church*:

> By her complete adherence to the Father's will, to His Son's redemptive work, and to every prompting of the Holy Spirit, the Virgin Mary is the Church's model of faith and charity. Thus she is a "preeminent and … wholly unique member of the Church"; indeed, she is the "exemplary realization" (*typus*) of the Church (#967).

Still, you might be wondering why we honor Mary as queen. Venerable Pope Pius XII first established the Memorial of the Queenship of Mary back in 1954. With Jesus as our King, it only stands to reason that His mother would serve as our queen. In the words of Pope Benedict XVI:

> The small and simple young girl of Nazareth became Queen of the world! This is one of the marvels that reveal God's Heart. Of course, Mary's queenship is totally relative to Christ's kingship. He is the Lord whom after the humiliation of death on the Cross the Father exalted above any other creation in Heaven and on earth and under the earth (cf. Phil 2:9-11). Through a design of grace, the Immaculate Mother was fully associated with the mystery of the Son: in His Incarnation; in His earthly life, at first hidden at Nazareth and then manifested in the messianic ministry; in His Passion and death; and finally, in the glory of His Resurrection and Ascension into Heaven. [24]

The Blessed Mother is a monarch who serves with distinction and love. As Pope Benedict further stated:

> Mary…is Queen in her service to God for humanity, she is a Queen of love who lives the gift of herself to God so as to enter into the plan of man's salvation. She answered the Angel: "Behold, I am the handmaid of the Lord" (cf. Lk 1:38) and in the Magnificat she sings: God has regarded the low estate of His handmaiden (cf Lk 1:48). She

> helps us. She is Queen precisely by loving us, by helping us in our every need; she is our sister, a humble handmaid.[25]

Pope Benedict adds that Mary exercises her queenship of service by watching over us. From a young age, I felt as if the Blessed Mother were standing guard, making sure that my family was protected. The late Holy Father recognizes that we can trust Mary with our very lives:

> Through the Virgin Mary let us turn with trust to the One Who rules the world and holds in His Hand the future of the universe. For centuries she has been invoked as the celestial Queen of Heaven; in the Litany of Loreto after the prayer of the holy Rosary, she is implored eight times: as Queen of Angels, of Patriarchs, of Prophets, of Apostles, of Martyrs, of Confessors, of Virgins, of all the Saints and of Families. The rhythm of these ancient invocations and daily prayers, such as the *Salve Regina*, help us to understand that the Blessed Virgin, as our Mother beside her Son Jesus in the glory of Heaven, is always with us in the daily events of our life.
>
> The title "Queen" is thus a title of trust, joy and love. And we know that the One who holds a part of the world's destinies

> in her hand is good, that she loves us and helps us in our difficulties.[26]

Ironically, I have found that the more I meditate on Mary's role as queen, the closer I become to her. She reigns in my mind and in my heart, and I cannot help but grow in love, not only for her, but for her Son, Jesus. I pray that you, too, will experience a special relationship with the queen who reigns both in Heaven and on earth.

I would like to offer a special word of encouragement to those who have had difficulty accepting Mary as mother. Take the situation to prayer, knowing that God is ready to assist you. He is prepared to open your mind and your heart to the love of Mary.

While we recognize Mary as queen, she is not a goddess. She is a created being, not a divine being — sanctified by the Holy Spirit, but every bit a creature of God, just as you and I are. Mary is not to be worshipped. However, as the mother of the Savior, she holds a special place in the Church — and should in our hearts as well.

Personal Reflections:

1. How do you relate to Mary as queen?
2. Can you point to instances in your life where you felt Mary's queenly protection?
3. How has Mary come to your aid in recent weeks?
4. How can you demonstrate your trust in Mary this week?

CHAPTER 19
Growing in Virtue: Eternal Happiness

During a particularly rough period in my life, I was attending a daily Mass when I heard the lovely strains of a hymn based on a reading from St. Paul's first letter to the Corinthians. To this day, when I read the Scripture passage, I am filled with awe:

> What eye has not seen, and ear has not heard, and what has not entered the human heart, what God has prepared for those who love him (1 Cor 2:9).

I think of the lovely sunsets I have witnessed … the breathtaking beauty of Ireland's Cliffs of Moher … and the elegance of the Pacific Ocean. And yet, as wonderful as those sights were, they do not compare with the beatific vision that awaits us in Heaven.

I think also of the soul-stirring sounds of a symphony … the poignancy of the music of *Les Misérables* … the gentle swish of the sea at night. And, as magnificent as those sounds might be, they pale in comparison to the soothing sounds of the heavenly realm.

We must grow in virtue to the point that eternal happiness awaits us. True, our soul may spend time in Purgatory to prepare for the celestial banquet, but

Heaven is our true destination. That is not to say that the climb to paradise is easy, but it is possible, thanks to the overwhelming mercy of God.

I am reminded here of the words of St. Thérèse of Lisieux, who described the desire for Heaven far better than I ever could:

> I always wanted to become a saint … Instead of being discouraged, I told myself that God would not make me wish for something impossible … I will look for some means of going to heaven by a little way which is very short and very straight. It is Your Arms, Jesus, which are the elevator to carry me to heaven. So there is no need for me to grow up. In fact, just the opposite: I must become less and less.[27]

The Little Flower had found an express route to Heaven in the loving arms of her Savior. Filled with a child-like faith, she had no need to worry. She exhibited a tremendous, unshakeable trust in Jesus which propelled her to the greatest heights of sanctity.

We can also take great comfort from St. Faustina's visions of Heaven, as described in her famous *Diary*:

> Today I was in heaven, in spirit, and I saw its unconceivable beauties and the happiness that awaits us after death. I saw how all creatures give ceaseless praise and glory

> to God. I saw how great is happiness in God, which spreads to all creatures, making them happy; and then all the glory and praise which springs from this happiness returns to its source; and they enter into the depths of God, contemplating the inner life of God, the Father, the Son, and the Holy Spirit, whom they will never comprehend of fathom.
>
> This source of happiness is unchanging in its essence, but it is always new, gushing forth happiness for all creatures.[28]

Saint Bernadette Soubirous was a humble soul, but she readily boasted of the glories of Heaven:

> My crown in heaven should shine with innocence and its flowers should be radiant as the sun. Sacrifices are the flowers Jesus and Mary chose.[29]

But perhaps the most comforting thought about Heaven comes courtesy of St. Thomas More, who said simply, "Earth hath no sorrow that heaven cannot heal."[30]

Personal Reflections

1. Take a few moments to ponder Heaven. Does thinking about Heaven increase your love for God?
2. How can you entrust yourself to Jesus today?
3. What does the concept of eternal happiness mean to you?
4. When you ponder the Coronation of Mary as queen of Heaven and earth, what thoughts come to mind?

CHAPTER 20
Saintly Encounters: St. Elizabeth Ann Seton

It was the dancing shoes that first caught my eye.

When I first visited the National Shrine of St. Elizabeth Ann Seton in Emmitsburg, Maryland, I was enchanted by the display of the distinguished saint's dancing shoes. They showed her love of entertainment and music, and I knew right then and there that I had found a fast friend in her.

Before that, I had limited knowledge of this incredible woman. I knew her canonization in 1975 to be a key event in the history of the United States. Churches and schools in my corner of the country took her as their namesake, and I realized she had special appeal for American women.

The more I read about the first American-born saint, the more fascinated I became. Her resilience in the wake of tragedy and trauma was truly inspiring. She was a force to be reckoned with — on or off the dance floor!

New York City-born in 1774, Elizabeth Ann Bayley was the daughter of Episcopalian parents. When she was just 19 years old, Elizabeth wed William Magee Seton, a prominent businessman.[31] In 1803, her husband died of tuberculosis; in the aftermath of the tragedy, Elizabeth entered the Catholic Church two years later.

When she moved to Emmitsburg in 1809, she founded her own religious order: the Sisters of Charity of St. Joseph. In addition, she launched what would become the beginnings of the U.S. Catholic school system, founding St. Joseph's Academy and Free School.

In reading the writings of St. Elizabeth Ann Seton, I have found that she offers a timeless wisdom that is especially appealing for those who face monumental hardships in their lives. For instance, she once wrote:

> I am satisfied to sow in tears if I may reap in joy. And when all the wintry storms of time are past, we shall enjoy the delights of an eternal spring.[32]

For those who find themselves in the midst of travails, St. Elizabeth Ann Seton offers these words of consolation:

> Go to Him with faith, love, and confidence — He will help. Fill yourself with His Spirit and He Himself will govern.[33]

Elizabeth's experience as both a biological mother and a spiritual mother connects her with Mary, the mother of Jesus. She knew first-hand what it was like to sacrifice for the sake of the children in her physical and spiritual care. She loved fiercely and passionately and provided a deep source of support for those who came to her for assistance.

She exhibited a profound trust in the Lord, on Whom she depended for everything:

> I resign the present and the future to Him Who is the Author and Conductor of both.[34]

May we imitate St. Elizabeth Ann Seton in her total trust in the Almighty, and allow Him to direct our steps into the future — a future which we hope includes everlasting life with Him!

Personal Reflections

1. Of the quotes attributed here to St. Elizabeth Ann Seton, which one resonates the most for you?
2. How can you follow Elizabeth's example and make a difference in the life of a young person this week?
3. What difficulty are you facing that you need to turn over to the Lord?
4. Think of one way you can demonstrate spiritual motherhood or fatherhood this week.

CONCLUSION
Glorious Encounters on the Go

You may long for a glorious encounter with Mary, but you find yourself pressed for time. Between your job and family responsibilities, it may be hard to work in a meaningful conversation with Our Lady.

The beautiful thing is, Mary knows your struggles. After all, she served as a busy wife and mother during her time on earth. She recognizes that you may be short on time, and she is willing to meet you where you are, in the time crunch of your life.

Our encounters with Mary do not have to be long in order to be meaningful. Indeed, a glance in Mary's direction may be all it takes to spark a brief conversation which is the highlight of your day. The important thing is to spot the prayer opportunities which occur during a given day and to respond to them generously.

I used to become frustrated waiting in line — for anything! In college, I had been taught in my radio journalism classes that seconds count, and I did not want my seconds to add up to hours spent waiting. Waiting seemed like a tremendous waste of time — time which could be better spent in a variety of endeavors.

But, as I began to grow in my faith, I discovered that these waiting periods were, indeed, gifts from God. They were golden opportunities to take stock of my life … to ponder the beauty of God's creation … and to pray.

The more I began to take advantage of these holy moments, the more my frustration faded. Rather than becoming anxious, I grew calm and even content. These "dead periods" within my day transformed into invitations to meet with Mary. As a result, I went about my duties with more enthusiasm, knowing that she was right beside me.

Take, for instance, my weekly trips to the supermarket. It is a rare event when I can find a cashier free, so chances are high I will have to wait in line for my turn to pay for my goodies. Ordinarily, such down time would fill me with dread. However, I have now adopted a positive attitude about the wait. I may spend my wait time asking Mary to intercede for a blessed shopping trip … expressing thanks for my bounty … or remembering those who have asked me for prayer. I have found such prayer time to be much more rewarding than checking my email or scrolling through my social media feed. The time spent praying frees up my spirit so that I am more open to Mary and, in turn, to God and His will for my life.

A school parking lot may also provide a great opportunity to communicate with the Blessed Mother.

I can devote time to asking her to ask God to bless my family, our school, and our community. I can discuss with her whatever troubles me about my relationships, both inside and outside my household. At such times, I can recognize that Mary is my best friend and is always ready to listen to my needs and the desires of my heart.

Even an errand known for marathon wait times — such as a trip to get my driver's license renewed — can bring with it a host of blessings. The time I spend waiting in line can be devoted to praying a Rosary for the Holy Souls in Purgatory. As I repeat the prayers in my head, I can bring to mind the names of family members and friends who have died. Knowing that I am providing some spiritual assistance to them can be a soul-lifting experience.

Praying during our wait times can aid us in our efforts to draw closer to Mary. Any good and fruitful relationship takes time to blossom. That is also true for our relationship with the mother of Jesus. We need to spend time with her in order to grow in love of her and of our neighbor. The more we focus the eyes of our soul on Mary rather than on our troubles, the more we develop our faith. Mary becomes our compass, enabling us to navigate our world with confidence.

Sometimes, as I am waiting in line, I look around and spot an elderly man or woman waiting along with me. I reflect that the individual may have little time left in this world, and so each moment must be particularly dear for that person. None of us knows how much time we have left on earth, which makes it all the more imperative for us to use our time wisely.

As a result, I now look forward to my wait times, knowing that Mary is there in my midst. My errands become more pleasant and my spirit soars, as I realize that I have a chance to meet my beloved mother in the ordinary circumstances of my life.

The Vision That Awaits Us

If only we open our eyes and our hearts, we will see glimpses of the glory that is Heaven throughout our days. They may come through a child's smile … an elegant seaside view … or the glistening stars in the night sky. As we go about our daily lives, Mary can be our chief cheerleader, helping us to discover the path that will lead to eternal bliss. We can trust her to guide us and sustain us during our earthly journey.

The 16 years that I waited for my beautiful prayer to be answered were not wasted. During that time, I grew a deeper love for Mary, one I draw upon each day to help me weather the storms of life. My longing to see my daughter face-to-face brought about a patience and resilience that have drawn me closer to Jesus — the love of my life.

I wish the same joy for you as you travel along life's highway. And I hope someday that you will see the face of Mary, smiling gently upon you as she leads you to your heavenly home, where sorrows will be but a memory and lasting happiness will be your constant companion.

The glories of Heaven and of God know no bounds. As it states in Psalm 145:

> One generation praises your deeds to the next
> And proclaims your mighty works.
> They speak of the splendor of your majestic glory,
> Tell of your wonderful deeds.

It is this glorious vision that awaits us when we cooperate with God's magnificent plan. May the same Lord Who paints the sunrise across the canvas of the sky make of you a masterpiece of His love.

Personal Reflections

1. How could you re-order your week to make room for glorious encounters with Mary?
2. What is your go-to prayer when you are on the run?
3. Do you become frustrated when you have to wait? If so, take this concern to prayer, knowing that God stands ready to assist you.
4. How can you bring Mary along with you in your travels?

Additional Rosary Resources

HELPFUL VIDEOS

Father Chris Alar, MIC:

"Explaining the Faith: Understanding Mary: How to Explain Her Role." DivineMercyPlus.org/videos/mary-mother-god

"Explaining the Faith: The Role of Mary: The Assumption, Coronation, Etc." DivineMercyPlus.org/videos/role-mary

"Mary the Mother of Mercy." www.YouTube.com/watch?v=EWJBa5qbFzc

Father Donald Calloway, MIC:

"The Virgin Mary in Our Lives." www.YouTube.com/watch?v=YPYKftebVwY

"The Virgin Mary: The Masterpiece of God." www.YouTube.com/watch?v=hhdAiEVme0I

ENLIGHTENING PODCASTS

"Catholic Momcast." www.CatholicMom.com/catholic-momcast.

"Catholic Saints with Fr. Dan Cambra, MIC." DivineMercyPlus.org/podcast/catholic-saints-fr-dan

"Explaining the Faith with Fr. Chris Alar, MIC." DivineMercyPlus.org/podcast/explaining-faith-fr-chris-alar

"How They Love Mary with Fr. Edward Looney." podcasts.Apple.com/us/podcast/how-they-love-mary/id1458192119

"Sparks of Mercy with Chris Sparks." DivineMercyPlus.org/podcast/sparks-mercy

INSIGHTFUL BOOKS

Father Donald Calloway, MIC. *10 Wonders of the Rosary.* Marian Press: 2019.

____________________. *Champions of the Rosary: The History and Heroes of a Spiritual Weapon.* Marian Press: 2016.

____________________. *Marian Gems: Daily Wisdom on Our Lady.* Marian Press: 2014.

____________________. *Under the Mantle: Marian Thoughts from a 21st Century Priest.* Marian Press: 2013.

Father Michael Gaitley, MIC. *33 Days to Morning Glory: Group Retreat & Study Guide: A Do-It-Yourself Retreat in Preparation for Marian Consecration.* Marian Press: 2023.

Maria V. Gallagher. *Joyful Encounters with Mary: A Woman's Guide to Living the Mysteries of the Rosary.* Marian Press: 2022.

Father Thaddaeus Lancton, MIC. *Shining in Spotless Splendor: Consecration to the Immaculate Conception.* Marian Press, 2023.

Acknowledgments

I give all praise to God for the abundance of blessings He has poured forth into my life.

To the Blessed Mother, my sincerest thanks for welcoming me as your child and providing the guiding star for my writing. You have shown me the path to salvation.

To the team at Marian Press, especially Dr. Joe McAleer, Chris Sparks, and Dr. Robert Stackpole, thank you for your skillful shepherding of this labor of love to publication. I am deeply indebted to you for your continuing enthusiasm for my work.

To my co-workers in the cause of defending life, my heartfelt gratitude for your unwavering support. You have helped me more than you will ever know.

To the indomitable ladies of my Cursillo prayer group, I wish you many glorious encounters with Mary and all the saints. You inspire me every day.

To my beloved daughter, Gabriella, thank you for being the greatest blessing that God ever bestowed upon me. I love you from the depths of my being.

About the Author

Maria V. Gallagher is an author, speaker, life coach, and advocate for pregnant women and their children. Her previous books include *Joyful Encounters with Mary: A Woman's Guide to Living the Mysteries of the Rosary* (Marian Press, 2022) and *Mercy's Power: Inspiration to Serve the Gospel of Life* (Marian Press, 2023).

A former radio news reporter and television news producer, Maria's journalistic work has been broadcast on *CBS Radio News* and *AP Radio News.* Her work also regularly appears on the *National Right to Life News Today* and *LifeNews.com* websites.

Maria credits *CatholicMom.com* for helping her hone her skills as a writer and as a mother. She holds an undergraduate degree in journalism from the Ohio State University and a graduate degree in journalism from Northwestern University.

Maria is an active member of her parish and the worldwide Cursillo movement and makes her home in central Pennsylvania. She is the mother of one beautiful ballerina and a mentor to many.

Notes

[1] For more on consecration to the Immaculate Heart of Mary, please see *33 Days to Morning Glory:Group Retreat & Study Guide: A Do-It-Yourself Retreat in Preparation for Marian Consecration* by Fr. Michael E. Gaitley (Marian Press, 2013).
[2] "After His Resurrection, Jesus Appeared First to Mary, Say the Saints." EWTN.com, https://ewtn.co.uk/article-after-his-resurrection-jesus-appeared-first-to-his-mother-mary-say-the-saints.
[3] Ibid.
[4] Ibid.
[5] Ibid.
[6] Ibid.
[7] Ibid.
[8] See the National Shrine of St. Rita of Cascia website: www.saintritashrine.org/pilgrimages-retreats.
[9] "Rita: Daughter, Wife, Mother, & Widow," The National Shrine of St. Rita of Cascia website: www.saintritashrine.org/saint-rita-of-cascia.
[10] Ibid.
[11] See *Catechism of the Catholic Church:* www.usccb.org/sites/default/files/flipbooks/catechism.
[12] *Laudate App*, Aycka Soft, developer.
[13] *Catechism* #966; Byzantine Liturgy, *Troparian,* Feast of the Dormition, August 15.
[14] Ven. Pope Pius XII, *Munificentissimus Deus*, Nov. 1, 1950: www.vatican.va/content/pius-xii/en/apost_constitutions/documents/hf_p-xii_apc_19501101_munificentissimus-deus.html.
[15] Ibid., 35.
[16] Ibid., 39.
[17] See: www.ewtn.com/catholicism/library/novena-of-our-lady-of-mount-carmel-9118
[18] "Litanies," EWTN.com: www.ewtn.com/catholicism/devotions/litanies-80.
[19] Ibid.
[20] "Litany of the Blessed Virgin," EWTN.com: www.ewtn.com/catholicism/devotions/litany-of-the-blessed-virgin-262
For more beautiful litanies of Our Lady, see *Shining in Spotless Splendor: Consecration to the Immaculate Conception* by Fr. Thaddaeus Lancton, MIC (Marian Press, 2023).
[21] "St. Monica: The Patron Saint of Mothers," The Basilica of

the National Shrine of the Immaculate Conception website: www.nationalshrine.org/blog/st-monica-the-patron-saint-of-mothers.
[22] Ibid.
[23] Ibid.
[24] See "Celebrating Mary's Queenship of Heaven and Earth," The Basilica of the National Shrine of the Immaculate Conception website: www.nationalshrine.org/blog/celebrating-marys-queenship-of-heaven-and-earth.
[25] Ibid.
[26] Pope Benedict XVI, General Audience, Aug. 22, 2012: www.vatican.va/content/benedict-xvi/en/audiences/2012/documents/hf_ben-xvi_aud_20120822.html.
[27] "St. Thérèse Novena Day Three: Jesus Lift Me," Society of the Little Flower website: www.littleflower.org/prayers/nine-day-novena/st-therese-novena-day-three-jesus-lift
[28] Saint Maria Faustina Kowalska, *Divine Mercy in My Soul* (Stockbridge, Massachusetts: Marian Press, 1987), #777.
[29] "10 Quotes from the Saints on What Heaven Will be Like," Aleteia, https://aleteia.org/2015/11/12/10-quotes-from-the-saints-on-what-heaven-will-be-like.
[30] Ibid.
[31] "Saint Elizabeth Ann Seton Biography," The National Shrine of St. Elizabeth Ann Seton website: https://setonshrine.org/wp-content/uploads/2018/08/Saint-Elizabeth-Ann-Seton-Biography.pdf.
[32] "Quotes of St. Elizabeth Ann Seton," The National Shrine of St. Elizabeth Ann Seton website: https://setonshrine.org/wp-content/uploads/2020/03/St-Elizabeth-Ann-Seton-Quotes.pdf.
[33] Ibid.
[34] Ibid.

More from Maria Gallagher

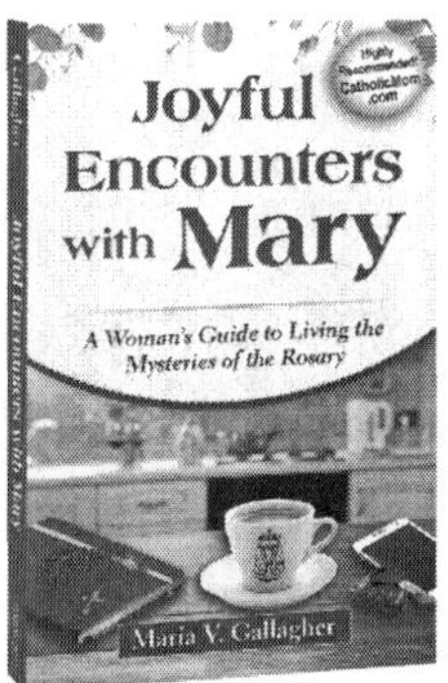

Y120-JYMY
Paperback / 164 pages

Joyful Encounters with Mary

A Woman's Guide to Living the Mysteries of the Rosary

Amid life's daily struggles, one can find true joy in encountering and loving the Blessed Mother and, in turn, encountering and loving her Son. We can relate to Mary as not only mother but friend, based on our mutual experiences with the mysteries of life. *Joyful Encounters with Mary* speaks of the power that can be unleashed when one surrenders to God's sometimes mystifying plan. While facing various challenges — from birthing a baby to birthing a project — we can experience a peace that surpasses all understanding and leads to incomparable joy.

Y120-MPOW
Paperback / 156 pages

Mercy's Power

Inspiration to Serve the Gospel of Life

This is a critical time in the history of our world and of our faith — a time when advocates for life must be more persuasive and courageous than ever before. As a result, we need a spiritual guidebook, one that can provide solace and support during these turbulent times. We require a handbook for how best to renew the culture of life in an environment that can be quite hostile to our message. While *Roe v. Wade* is now history, a range of threats to innocent human life — from the moment of conception to the twilight of life — persist.

For our complete line of books, prayer cards, pamphlets, and more, visit ShopMercy.org or call 1-800-462-7426.

Join the

Association of Marian Helpers,

headquartered at the
National Shrine of The Divine Mercy,
and share in special blessings!

An invitation from
Fr. Joseph, MIC, director

Marian Helpers is an Association of Christian faithful of the Congregation of Marian Fathers of the Immaculate Conception. By becoming a member, you share in the spiritual benefits of the daily Masses, prayers, and good works of the Marian priests and brothers.

This is a special offer of grace given to you by the Church through the Marian Fathers. Please consider this opportunity to share in these blessings, along with others whom you would wish to join into this spiritual communion.

1-800-462-7426 • Marian.org/join